Cambridge Elements

Elements in the Gothic
edited by
Dale Townshend
Manchester Metropolitan University
Angela Wright
University of Sheffield

DISABILITY AND THE GOTHIC

The Nineteenth Century

Essaka Joshua
University of Notre Dame

Shaftesbury Road, Cambridge CB2 8EA, United Kingdom

One Liberty Plaza, 20th Floor, New York, NY 10006, USA

477 Williamstown Road, Port Melbourne, VIC 3207, Australia

314–321, 3rd Floor, Plot 3, Splendor Forum, Jasola District Centre,
New Delhi – 110025, India

Cambridge University Press is part of Cambridge University Press & Assessment,
a department of the University of Cambridge.

We share the University's mission to contribute to society through the pursuit of
education, learning and research at the highest international levels of excellence.

www.cambridge.org
Information on this title: www.cambridge.org/9781009669542

DOI: 10.1017/9781009300865

© Essaka Joshua 2026

This publication is in copyright. Subject to statutory exception and to the provisions
of relevant collective licensing agreements, no reproduction of any part may take
place without the written permission of Cambridge University Press & Assessment.

When citing this work, please include a reference to the DOI 10.1017/9781009300865

First published 2026

A catalogue record for this publication is available from the British Library

*A Cataloging-in-Publication data record for this Element is available from the Library
of Congress*

ISBN 978-1-009-66954-2 Hardback
ISBN 978-1-009-30090-2 Paperback
ISSN 2634-8721 (online)
ISSN 2634-8713 (print)

Cambridge University Press & Assessment has no responsibility for the persistence
or accuracy of URLs for external or third-party internet websites referred to in this
publication and does not guarantee that any content on such websites is, or will remain,
accurate or appropriate.

For EU product safety concerns, contact us at Calle de José Abascal, 56, 1°, 28003
Madrid, Spain, or email eugpsr@cambridge.org

Disability and the Gothic

The Nineteenth Century

Elements in the Gothic

DOI: 10.1017/9781009300865
First published online: February 2026

Essaka Joshua
University of Notre Dame

Author for correspondence: Essaka Joshua, ejoshua@nd.edu

Abstract: Disability is central to the Gothic imagination. This Element draws together disability and Gothic literature in ways that show the interplay between them. The first chapter offers a brief history of Critical Disability Studies, and the manner in which Gothic has been integral to the evolution of disability theory. It shows the increasing centrality of the Gothic to the development of Critical Disability Studies, and describes the emergence of the subfield of Gothic Disability Studies. The second chapter and third chapters offer close readings of particular texts, showing how Gothic bodies and minds articulate and shift their relationship to the aesthetic and affective frameworks of the nineteenth century. While disability sometimes represents the 'other' in Gothic literature, this positioning far from exhausts the ways in which disability is presented in this genre.

Keywords: disability, Gothic, madness, Victorian, Romantic

© Essaka Joshua 2026

ISBNs: 9781009669542 (HB), 9781009300902 (PB), 9781009300865 (OC)
ISSNs: 2634-8721 (online), 2634-8713 (print)

Contents

1 Disability Studies and the Gothic   1

2 Disability and the Gothic Body   22

3 Gothic Madness and Neurodiversity   40

4 Reclaiming Gothic: Concluding Questions   62

    References   63

1 Disability Studies and the Gothic

Disability is present in Gothic literature in ways that are unique. Mad scientists, deformed monsters, and threats of bodily and mental harm are all familiar features of the genre. Indeed, Gothic literature often depends for its effectiveness on readers' fears about disabled bodies and minds. This Element investigates the role Gothic plays in our understanding of disability, and the importance of disability for the Gothic.

Beginning with an account of the place of Gothic in the fundamentals of disability theory, Section 1 presents a critical and theoretical history of the Gothic in Critical Disability Studies (the theoretical branch of Disability Studies). The first part of this introduction focuses on the role of Gothic in work by scholars largely outside Romantic and Victorian Studies; the second part provides an outline of the development of Gothic Disability Studies as a subfield within Romantic and Victorian Disability Studies. Disability Studies approaches to Gothic literature initially focused on problematic uses of disability, but scholars have increasingly moved in the direction of reclaiming, or reframing, our understanding of the Gothic. This section addresses the uses of Gothic by period and non-period specialists in order to trace how Gothic became emblematic of problematic accounts of disability, and the subsequent development of Gothic Disability Studies into a subfield.

My definition of Gothic centres on shared motifs (characters; plots; locations; objects; and narrative forms) that reach across genres, as well as the genre, Gothic. In terms of Gothic characters, I include revenants, tyrants, and victims; those who are sceptical of the supernatural and those (human or animal) who corroborate it; warner characters, who are custodians of folklore and legend; and uncanny characters. Gothic includes the past in some sense returning, the display of unusual or non-normative mental and bodily states, and the changing of bodies through penetration, death, injury, disease, or dismemberment. There are mystery plots, threats and rescues, transgression and punishment, tales about tales, and identity-driven plots, in which standard categories are challenged. The supernatural takes many forms in the Gothic, but it is usually marked by the disruption of cause and effect – banging with no source, or a vampire with no reflection. Gothic objects return with a satisfying frequency: locked boxes, ancestral paintings, tapestries, books, lights, beds, safe objects, and objects of danger. Motivations are also motifs. For instance, why do characters enter haunted houses? There are multiple reasons, including curiosity, necessity, obligation, disbelief, accident, and invitation. Gothic locations range from the Medieval castle to the suburban villa, and from the forest to the sea. Though they are quite varied, they share characteristics, such as decay, isolation, confusion, or confinement. Gothic space can be convoluted and labyrinthine, or it can be transitional, such as marshes and borderlands. It can be subterranean or attic space, and, unlike much non-Gothic nineteenth-century literature, it frequently reminds us that there are bedrooms. Within Gothic spaces, entryways and other kinds of transitional space, such as staircases are suggestive of liminality. Outside, Gothic mists, fog, storms, and twilight present us with indeterminate binaries, redolent of unpredictability and danger. Narrative structures in Gothic literature are also shared. The frame narrative gives us stories within stories, with safety frames (where the character lives to tell the tale), and dangerous frames (where they do not or their fate is unknown). The haunted house tale is tripartite: the characters enter the space; they encounter what is there; they leave. Gothic motifs are the essence of this genre and are central to its metatextual engagement. Gothic texts are never far from other Gothic texts.

This Element will focus on a variety of critical methods within Disability Studies, demonstrating how we might approach disability in Gothic literature and what is to be gained from this theoretical position. I have included a mixture of canonical and non-canonical writers from across the century, a range of genres (poetry, novels, short stories), and a variety of modes (e.g., classical, imperialist, sensationalist, rural) in order reflect the diversity of Gothic engagement with disability. This Element deliberately avoids well-worn territory, such as the madwoman in the attic and Frankenstein's creature, in order to make the case that engagement with disability in the Gothic is extensive, and to encourage others to find more.[1] The eclecticism in the choice of material presents some challenges to coherence, especially in the short-form monograph; but, in addition to the reasons mentioned earlier, these texts are chosen to facilitate readings that introduce the theoretical underpinnings of Disability Studies.

The Cambridge Elements series allows for short sections that present brief and accessible readings. This methodology, it is hoped, will encourage new conversations for scholars of Gothic literature. I have included discussion of a number of short stories because these are often neglected in Gothic scholarship and teaching. As Victoria Margree (2018: 163) points out, 'this is in part due to the ephemeral nature of the periodical publishing in which it often appeared, but it is also a result of the critical bias of twentieth-century canon

---

[1] As I have published a chapter and an article on disability and *Frankenstein*, and there is extensive consideration of this novel within Disability Studies, I shall refer the reader to this and other Disability Studies work on *Frankenstein*. See Davis, 1995; Gigante, 2000; Mossman, 2001; Krentz, 2004; Marchbanks, 2010; Joshua, 2011; Rodas, 2016; Wang, 2017; Botting, 2018; Holmes, 2018; Richman, 2018; Wallace, 2020; Knight, 2020; Joshua, 2020; Bodammer, 2025. As there is so much Disability Studies scholarship on *Frankenstein*, some consideration of this text will be incorporated via the survey of this scholarship.

builders who deemed the short story an inferior form'.[2] Short stories deserve more attention than they currently receive because they are deeply embedded within the genre and its modes, and their size enables readers to rapidly discover the complexity and range of Gothic literature. I hope that the eclecticism of the choice of texts is to some extent mitigated by the coherence of the Gothic. Gothic texts work within a tradition, and are in conversation with each other. This Element is more about how this conversation incorporates disability than about surveying how early nineteenth-century Gothic differs from late.

1.1 Gothic and Early Disability Studies

In the 1970s and 1980s, the earliest stirrings of Gothic Disability Studies are evident both in the foundational work of Critical Disability Studies and in the surveys on disability and literature. Gothic texts are used in both types of study to demonstrate and illustrate that disability is commonly identified as horrific or freakish in literature and culture. Early Disability Studies concentrated on exposing ableist tropes and lamented their metaphorical and symbolic implications. These accounts of literature were often connected to broader claims about the endemic cultural prevalence of problematic characterization, plots, and imagery.

Critical Disability Studies offers important theoretical frameworks for understanding disability; it is also sometimes work that comments on literary texts. For the pioneering theorist Colin Barnes (1992: 19), for example, disabling stereotypes 'are fundamental to the discrimination and exploitation which disabled people encounter daily, and contribute significantly to their systematic exclusion from mainstream community life'. Barnes (1992: 12) dismisses *Frankenstein* as a tale of 'menace, mystery or deprivation' that uses disability to add atmosphere or arouse curiosity. Frankenstein's creature stands out as the most frequently discussed Gothic character in the early critical and theoretical work on disability in film, literature and culture, to the extent that he is as much emblematic of the early critical approaches to literary disability as he is of the Gothic genre as a whole.

The extent to which disabled characters symbolize problematic social or moral states troubles many early critics. Alan Gartner and Tom Joe's essay collection, *Images of the Disabled, Disabling Images* (1987) is one of the earliest books to address the problem of the disabling stereotype. Their study exposes the literary scapegoating and demonization of people with disabilities, and like Barnes, they view negative stereotypes as playing a significant role in

---

[2] For more on the position of the short story in the literary marketplace and the critical neglect of the genre, see Orel, 1986 and Magree, 2018.

social disablement and exclusionary cultures. Paul K. Longmore's comments on film and television in this collection are also relevant to literary study. Longmore (1987: 67) suggests that 'giving disabilities to villainous characters reflects and reinforces, albeit in exaggerated fashion, three common prejudices': 'disability is a punishment for evil; disabled people are embittered by their "fate"; and disabled people resent the nondisabled and would, if they could, destroy them'. Monster characters, he comments, are often treated as subhuman, 'depending on the extent of [their] disability', with 'the final and only possible solution' being death (Longmore, 1987: 689). Kriegel's essay on 'The Cripple in Literature' identifies a further Gothic type, concentrating on the varied uses of mobility impairment. Kriegel (1987: 34–5) defines the 'demonic cripple' as burning with 'his need for vengeance', and displaying a 'pervasive sense of absence' that prompts this need for revenge. This criticism of equivalence (often called the 'negative image' approach), where disability in literature is interpreted figuratively, was later superseded by political, cultural, and identity-based theories of disability.

The 'negative image' approach was found wanting in several respects by later critics. For example, it did not immediately produce a new theorizing of disability. The latter came about through the redefinition of disability in the social sciences, and by activist movements. The social-barriers or social-interaction approach to disability, known as the *social model*, was one of the earliest alternatives to the idea of intrinsic or medicalized disability or the *medical model*.[3] As Simi Linton (1997: 224) observes, the medical definition of disability 'casts human variation as deviance from the norm, as a pathological condition, as deficit, and, significantly, as an individual burden and personal tragedy'. It assumes that disability is caused by an individual's body or mind. The social model, however, suggests that disability arises contextually. Michael Oliver's historical study of the distinction between the individual and social dimensions of disability, *The Politics of Disablement* (1990), is an important development of this theory, and remains influential in literary studies and in policymaking today. According to Colin Barnes and Geof Mercer (1997: 1), the social model of disability examines 'how socially constructed barriers (for example, in the design of buildings, modes of transport and communication, and discriminatory attitudes) have "disabled" people'. This approach differentiates bodily conditions that limit function (*impairments*) from the disadvantages associated with them (*disabilities*). The distinction is useful because it recognizes that disability is dynamic and

---

[3] Michael Oliver and Colin Barnes (2012: 54) note that the social model was intended to be 'an analytical framework and not an empirical social theory', suggesting that it is not a model in the usual sense.

context dependent. The activism and collective action of the 1970s and 1980s culminated in the passing of the Americans with Disabilities Act (ADA) in 1990 and the 1995 Disability Discrimination Act (DDA) in the UK, legislation that had global repercussions.[4]

Aside from the impairment–disability distinction (*social model*), Oliver also made the case that disability is produced by a culture of individualism which, when combined with a capitalist economy, pushed disabled people to the margins of society and institutionalized those who could not labour in conventional ways. The ideology of individualism positions disability, Oliver claims, as a product both of ideology and of economic structures. The ideology of individualism, he suggests, causes people to think about disability solely in medical contexts, and presents 'the disabled individual as less than or more than human' (Oliver, 1990: 61). Oliver regards culture as implicated in the formation of disabled identities, arguing that disability stereotypes are largely dehumanizing or sentimental. Significantly, he admits, however, that there had hitherto 'been little attempt to present the collective experience of disability culturally, and hence the process of identity formation for disabled individuals has usually been constrained by images of superheroes or pathetic victims' (Oliver, 1990: 62). While the early discussions of the social model do not engage directly with Gothic literature, Oliver recognized the importance of dehumanizing stereotypes and that there was important work for literary critics, contemporary writers, and artists to do.

In the mid-1990s, accepting the premise of the disability–impairment distinction, critics and theorists were next drawn towards thinking further about how disability concepts are formed. Tom Shakespeare's work is at the vanguard of the attempt to connect two important subdisciplines of Disability Studies: literary studies and sociology. Shakespeare (1994: 289) suggests that social theorists, like Oliver and others, neglected the cultural representation of disability because they were interested in a materialist understanding of disability derived from a 'Marxist conception of ideology', where 'ideas about disabled people' were treated as consequences of their material relations and of their 'socio-economic relationships'. Shakespeare argues that ideology alone is an 'inadequate tool for understanding disabling imagery and representation', and that cultural anthropology tends to ignore material origins. He calls instead for a combined approach, where interpersonal prejudice and prejudice 'implicit in cultural representation, in language and in socialization' are understood in relation to a materialist causality (Shakespeare, 1994: 296). For Shakespeare, however, the crux of the issue is psychological (Shakespeare, 1994: 297, 287):

---

[4] See UPIAS, "Fundamental Principles of Disability," 1976, pp. 3–4, cited in Oliver 1990: 11.

'disabled people remind non-disabled people of their own vulnerability', and so 'disabled people become ciphers for those feelings, processes or characteristics with which non-disabled society cannot deal'. While he does not discuss individual literary texts, Shakespeare asserts that disabled people are 'dustbins' for the 'disavowal' of non-disabled people's 'unease at their [own] physicality and mortality', and that this dominates the cultural presence of disability. He sums this up by citing Paul Longmore's comment that, '"as with popular portrayals of other minorities, the unacknowledged hostile fantasies of the stigmatizers are transferred to the stigmatized"' (Shakespeare, 1994: 298; citing Longmore, 1987: 67).

Additionally, Shakespeare (1994: 292) outlines the many ways in which Disability Studies can learn from feminist theory, suggesting 'that there is a general process by which the subordinated person becomes "the other", common to a range of groups in society: women, black people, and also disabled people', and, further, that the ways in which women's bodies are othered are pertinent for disabled bodies. Disabled people are othered, he argues, 'by virtue of their connection to nature; their visibility as evidence of the constraining body; and their status as constant reminders of mortality' (Shakespeare, 1994: 292). Alongside the binary opposition that othering is based on, Shakespeare also offers the idea of the *anomaly*, derived from the work of the anthropologist Mary Douglas, as a way to understand prejudice. Douglas argues that responses to anomalies – anything that lies outside our experience – are a fundamental building block for creating order. This, Shakespeare suggests, is why we have different reactions to temporary impairments from those we have for disabilities. Gothic literature briefly features in Shakespeare's analysis via his coopting of the idea of liminality from Frank Turner's work *The Ritual Process* (1969). 'Disabled people,' he writes, 'are seen to be ambiguous because they hover between humanity and animality, life and death, subjectivity and objectivity' (Shakespeare, 1994: 295). While these early sociological and anthropological studies tend not to name specific nineteenth-century texts, they are nevertheless concerned with the negative effects of literature that uses Gothic or frightening imagery.

Lennard J. Davis, Rosemarie Garland Thomson, and Michael Bérubé are some of the earliest critics and theorists to shift the discussion of disability towards the discursive practices and cultures surrounding and forming our notions of disability. Davis (1995: 49) asserts, in *Enforcing Normalcy*, for instance, that 'characters with disabilities are always marked with ideological meaning, as are moments of disease or accident that transform such characters'. Davis (1995: 23–4) centralizes the concept of normalcy, arguing that 'to understand the disabled body, one must return to the problem of the norm, the normal body', because norms 'create the "problem" of the disabled person'. Normalcy is important for literature, Davis (1995: 41) observes, because 'the very structures on which the novel rests tend to be normative, ideologically emphasizing the universal quality of the central character whose normativity encourages us to identify with him or her'. Drawing on the work of the sociologist Erving Goffman, Davis (1995: 29) argues that where norms are 'operative, then people with disabilities will be thought of as deviants'. Davis's influential work connects Foucault's ideas about power with the idea that industrialization marginalized people with disabilities. Foucault suggests, in *Discipline and Punish* (1975), that during the transition to a modern society at the end of the eighteenth century, the body appeared to be controlled through a range of disciplinary practices that make it normatively self-sufficient and productive. Foucault (1975: 184) argues that, 'like surveillance, and with it, normalization becomes one of the great instruments of power at the end of the classical age'. Foucauldian thinking dominates 1990s Disability Studies, as critics grappled with the nature of the contextual control that the disability–impairment distinction makes apparent.

Davis (1995: 144) raises several important questions about Gothic uses of the body and, particularly, its framing of the body as 'a zone of repulsion'. His central question about *Frankenstein* (and for his study as a whole) is: 'why does a physical difference produce such a profound response?' (Davis, 1995: 144). Davis offers two answers that are grounded in psychoanalytic theory. Firstly, that the revulsion comes less from the visual experience of the creature's physiognomy, and more from 'what that appearance suggests': the '*corps morcelé*' or fragmented body. Secondly, that the horror derives from 'a threat of touching, of being touched' – a threat that 'always initiates a dialectic of attraction and repulsion, of fear, hatred, or erotic attraction' (Davis, 1995: 145). Drawing on Freud and Lacan, Davis suggests that the disabled body appears to be disruptive because it is an uncanny reminder of the illusion of wholeness – a reminder that brings to the surface a repressed sense of the self as a fragmented body. The fragmented body is, for Davis, a repressed double, and the idea of the whole body (*Gestalt*) is held together by an act of will that is merely an hallucination. According to Davis, the *Gestalt* body is always threatening to fall apart. Davis implies here an expansive definition of disability: we are all disabled in the sense that disability is the basis of the normative body. The latter is an illusion we develop when we have repressed the fragmentary *unheimlich* body. Davis's analogy for this illusion is the Venus de Milo. This is a statue of a beautiful woman without arms that is nevertheless treated as if it were whole. The normate ideal is similarly an unstable 'phantom goddess of wholeness, normalcy, and unity', and it 'always exists in a dialectical play with the disabled body' that he characterizes as Medusa-like (Davis, 1995: 141, 157). Conventions of looking are such that we do not notice that the Venus de Milo's body is incomplete.

Like Davis, Rosemarie Garland Thomson (1997: 5) also called for literary criticism to move 'beyond assailing stereotypes', and to examine 'the conventions of representation' that produce identity 'within the social narratives of bodily differences'. In *Extraordinary Bodies*, Thomson (1997: 8, 15) offers the idea that the 'disabled figure' is a fictional entity that opens up 'a critical gap' between fictional and real people. The disabled figure, for Thomson (1997: 9), is 'informed more by received attitudes than [by] people's actual experience of disability', and it 'finds a home within the conventions and codes of literary representation'. The disabled figure contrasts with its opposite, the 'normate', with which it is mutually constituted. Thomson (1997: 8) explains that the term 'normate' 'designates the social figure through which people can represent themselves as definitive human beings'.[5] This new term creates a deliberate distancing from the problematic term 'normal' by reminding us of its constructed nature. Like the critics before her, Thomson (1997: 7) finds that disability is 'on the margins of fiction', and that 'corporeal departures from dominant expectations never go uninterpreted or unpunished, and conformities are almost always rewarded'.

Negative image approaches are also critiqued by David T. Mitchell and Sharon L. Snyder in *Narrative Prosthesis* (2000). They suggest that literature does not easily divide 'into "acceptable" and "unacceptable" representation', and that it is the job of the humanities to create 'a more sophisticated history of disability' that takes account of the 'textual performance of ever-shifting and unstable meanings' that occur during reading (Mitchell & Snyder, 2000: 42, 48). They describe disabled characters as, 'first, a stock feature of characterization, and second, as an opportunistic metaphorical device' acting as a narrative prosthesis that is a vehicle for 'an insatiable cultural fascination' with disability (Mitchell & Snyder, 2000: 47, 61). A prosthesis, Mitchell and Snyder (2000: 49) explain, is a 'crutch upon which literary narratives lean for their representational power, disruptive potentiality, and analytical insight'. This prosthesis attempts 'to accomplish an erasure of difference', but ultimately 'it fails in its primary objective: to return the incomplete body to the invisible status of a normative essence' (Mitchell & Snyder, 2000: 7, 8). The prosthetic use of disability in literature is, according to Mitchell and Snyder (2000: 51), a *'discursive dependency'*.

---

[5] Thomson credits this term to Daryl Evans, who used it in an informal talk to the Society for Disability Studies annual conference in Denver in 1989 (p. 140 n.60).

In their brief comments on *Frankenstein*, Mitchell and Snyder read the novel as an example where 'disability inaugurates narrative, but narrative inevitably punishes its own prurient interests by overseeing the extermination of the object of its fascination' (Mitchell & Snyder, 2000: 57). *Frankenstein* is for them, as it is for others, an uncanny 'return of the repressed' (Mitchell & Snyder, 2000: 132). But it is a return that represents a disabled subconscious, 'where the bearers of physical differences in literary history demand accountability from their literary primogenitors', and where 'those constructed as physically deviant assail those who would create them in that image' (Mitchell & Snyder, 2000: 132). The influence of arguments relating to narrative prosthesis and normalcy was felt throughout Disability Studies for the following decades and these theories remain important

The 1990s also inaugurated a great deal of research on monsters and freaks. Much of the theoretical work on monsters is relevant to discussions of disability. Jeffrey Jerome Cohen, in his essay collection *Monster Theory*, for instance, offers seven theses – on literary monsters from *Beowulf* to *Jurassic Park* – that have wider implications for Gothic Disability Studies. Cohen (1996: 4, 6, 20) suggests (1) that the monster is a 'cultural body' that is a product of its moment; (2) that monsters always escape; (3) that they signal a 'category crisis'; (4) that they embody difference; (5) that they police the borders of the possible; (6) that fear of a monster is really a form of desire; and (7) that monsters 'ask us to reevaluate our cultural assumptions about race, gender, sexuality, our perception of difference, our tolerance toward its expression'. Cohen defines monsters as creatures unbound by classification, and includes ghosts among them. We can see some connection with Disability Studies in Cohen's (1996: x) insistence that monsters should be 'understood as an embodiment of difference' rather than defined by doctors on the dissection table.[6]

Research on the historical presence of people who were known in the nineteenth century as 'freaks' is an additional avenue for studies of disability. Leslie Fiedler's *Freaks* is one of the earliest studies. Fiedler (1978: 16, 24) suggests that 'human curiosities' inspired both 'supernatural terror and natural sympathy' in 'mythic and mysterious' ways that go beyond the usual responses to disability. He reads early Gothic as preoccupied with psychological 'grotesques', rather than freaks, however (Fiedler, 1978: 262). Grotesques were 'people with psychological abnormalities like sado-masochism, incest, fratricide, and parricide' (Fiedler, 1978: 262). Fiedler (1978: 263–4) argues that *Frankenstein* introduced 'a new kind of Freak into the new genre' of science fiction 'in the Gothic mode'. Literature, on this reading, turns 'human prodigies

---

[6] See also Halberstam, 2000; Dittmer, 2023.

into metaphors for something else: the plight of the artist, the oppression of the poor, the terror of sexuality, or the illusory nature of social life' (Fiedler, 1978: 273). Fiedler (1978: 273) concludes, however, that literature gives little insight into 'what it is like to be a performer of one's own anomalous and inescapable fate'.

Building on this work, Rosemarie Garland Thomson's *Freakery* (1996) treats literary texts as part of a wider discourse of enfreakment that has its own rhetoric. This essay collection traces the exhibition cultures around nineteenth-century American freak shows. In her introduction, Thomson (1996: 3) characterizes the development in attitudes towards enfreaked people as a Comtean transition 'from a narrative of the marvelous to a narrative of the deviant'. Initially thought of as prodigious monsters, people with unusual disabilities in the theological phase of societies are later subjected to a pathologizing gaze in the modern scientific phase of societies. Importantly, Thomson (1996: 13) identifies a 'freak discourse' that 'did not vanish with the shows, but proliferated into a variety of contemporary discourses that still allude to its premises'. This discourse involved 'hyperbolic conventions of display' that emphasized the difference between the spectator and the performer via heightened sensationalized framing. As Thomson (1996: 5) suggests, 'freak discourse structured a cultural ritual that seized upon any deviation from the typical, embellishing and intensifying it to produce a human spectacle whose every somatic feature was laden with significance before the gaping spectator'. Freak discourse often involves juxtapositions of opposites, such as a giant and a dwarf, or includes figures that are hybrid (mermaid) or that are unusual, using exoticism and foreignness. Thomson (1996: 10) demonstrates that 'enfreakment emerges from cultural rituals that stylize, silence, differentiate, and distance the person whose bodies the freak-hunters or showmen colonize and commercialize'.

G. Thomas Couser treats Gothic rhetoric as one of several culturally prominent discourses of disability. He writes that Gothic rhetoric is present broadly in our culture and that it is derived 'from the fictional genre that so often features disfigured, deformed, or maimed characters' (Couser, 2009: 34).[7] Couser's interest is in the frequent use of Gothic rhetoric in disability autobiography. He describes the Gothic as preoccupied with disabilities that are 'characterized as literally a dreadful condition, to be shunned or avoided' (Couser, 2009: 34). Couser (2009: 34) observes that, at its worst, Gothic rhetoric encourages revulsion at disability, and, at its best, pity for the 'afflicted'. He suggests, moreover, that readers might find it surprising that disabled autobiographers use this language to describe themselves; but he explains that Gothic rhetoric is

---

[7] Aspects of this work appeared as Couser, 2001.

often a vehicle to voice a stage through which people pass. Gothic discourse is a common way to describe a rehabilitation process that moves from the shock of disablement towards acceptance or cure. Gothic rhetoric, then, characterizes a 'former condition as grotesque' and 'readers are invited to share narrators' relief at escaping marginalization' (Couser, 2009: 34). Used in this way, Couser (2009: 35) argues, Gothic rhetoric reinforces 'common attitudes towards disability – to evoke fear, dread, and revulsion'. It is also used to describe the fear of medical intervention, where medical care constitutes abuse, and procedures are painful. Gothic rhetoric, Couser (2009: 35) concludes, keeps 'conventional attitudes' towards disability in place.

Freak shows used a number of techniques of presentation that we see in Gothic literature. For instance, Gothic often contextualizes disability through warnings. The oral spiel performed by freakshow showmen, and printed pamphlets, similarly primed viewers for what was to come, fabricating exotic or far-fetched contexts that contextualized a performer's disabilities. In the freakshows, stage names and costuming emphasized monstrosity, and images accompanied displays stimulating curiosity. Brian Rosenberg (1996: 306) comments briefly, in this collection, on several nineteenth-century Gothic texts, such as H. G. Wells's *The Island of Dr. Moreau* (1896), from which he concludes that 'the freak becomes an embodiment of our darkest nightmares something alien not to be disturbed or challenged'. These ideas are later taken up by D. Christopher Gabbard (2012: 99) in his Disability Studies essay on *Jane Eyre*, where Edward Rochester presents his 'mad' wife to Jane with a showman's theatricality that conflates 'corporeal difference with teratology and demonology'.[8]

Ways of looking have been extensively theorized in the subfield of Visual Studies, and are prominent in discussions of literature and disability. Visual Studies examines the role of the gaze in disciplining, stigmatizing, gendering, sexualizing, colonizing, disabling, and racializing people. Thomson's *Staring* (2009), for instance, is informed by Foucault's *The Birth of the Clinic* (1963), and offers an important discussion of the ethical and definitional work involved in looking. Like Foucault, Thomson reveals the implied power relationships in interactions, and the exclusionary ideologies they support. Thomson's exploration of this topic draws special attention to the role that looking plays in the formation of disability. For her, staring is a discriminatory 'ocular intrusion' on 'people who cannot achieve inconspicuousness' (Thomson, 2009: 46). She includes Gothic literature in her brief discussion of Victor Hugo's *Notre Dame de Paris* (1831) and Charles Dickens's *A Christmas Carol* (1843),

---

[8] For more on Victorian freaks, see: Huff 2008; Tromp, 2009; Durvbach, 2009; Craton, 2009.

singling out Quasimodo and Tiny Tim as 'pathetic and romanticized' examples of disabled otherness (Thomson, 1997: 10). Thomson (1997: 9–10) suggests that critics tend to interpret disabled characters 'metaphorically or aesthetically without political awareness as conventional elements of the sentimental, romantic, Gothic, or grotesque traditions'.[9] She advocates sensitizing readers to the consequences of these elements.

Gothic appears in the foundational theoretical and critical work undertaken within Disability Studies from the 1970s onwards, as scholars use it to illustrate the cultural presence of disability as monstrous, frightening, or freakish. Critics note the widespread use of disabling stereotypes in canonical Gothic texts, such as *Frankenstein* and *A Christmas Carol*, often connecting them to wider concerns about the impact of the Gothic on the lives of disabled people. As Disability Studies matured, critics moved away from claims about Gothic metaphors and symbols to focus more on disability as a relational phenomenon, with discussion moving to socio-economic systems and discourses of disability. The field drew broadly from sociology, psychology, and feminist theory to investigate the marginal positioning of disability as a site for the projection of anxieties and stigma. The Gothic mode's emphasis on liminality and difference made it particularly attractive for these critics who investigated social exclusion. Gothic is recognized in early Disability Studies as a powerful cultural script that expresses anxieties about disabled bodies and minds.

1.2 Gothic Disability Studies: A Field

It was not until the second decade of the twenty-first century that serious consideration was given to Disability Studies' perspectives on Gothic literature by critics working in Gothic Studies. This prior lack of detailed consideration of Gothic disability has been remarked upon by several critics. Alan Gregory (2018: 292) noted, for instance, 'the sparsity of scholarly considerations of disability' in horror and Gothic. Ria Cheyne (2019: 29) speculated on why this might be. For her, 'disability's entrenched associations with both fear and vulnerability have attained it a central, though rarely acknowledged, position in the horror tradition'. Cheyne (2019: 29–30) expresses concern at the centrality of disability in Gothic horror, reminding us of the extent of the use of disability in icons of the genre, such as 'the deformed monster, the vulnerable blind or deaf character, the psychotic villain, and the protagonist (often female) teetering on the brink of madness'. I would add that a critical mass of disability theory needed to have been worked through before Gothic could be engaged with in ways that were productive.

---

[9] For more on this, see: Abram, 2022.

From the mid-2000s, however, the important theoretical and critical groundwork provided by first-wave Disability Studies prompted several extensive critical explorations of disability in Gothic literature of the Romantic period,[10] the Victorian period,[11] and the nineteenth century as a whole.[12] In the following years, there were two additional important landmarks in the field of Gothic Disability Studies, Ruth Bienstock Anolik's multi-authored essay collection, *Demons of the Body and Mind* (2010), the first book-length study to focus on Gothic literature, and Stevi Costa's 2018 special issue of *Studies in Gothic Fiction* on disabled Gothic bodies. Both focused attention on a range of texts from early to contemporary Gothic.

A prominent avenue of exploration from the early 2000s consisted in discourses of disability in Gothic literature, both in the postmodern sense and in more traditional rhetorical studies. Working with postmodern concepts, David Punter (2000: 39) argued that 'there are elements in the Gothic tradition that can be critically developed by bearing in mind the discourse of disability'. Punter (2000: 40) proposed a number of further routes for the exploration of disability within the Gothic: thus, Gothic is an uncanny 'return of those crippled or disabled forms that have been exiled, abjected'. Additionally, the disabled Gothic body is implicated in a postmodern disruption of meaning. For Punter (2000: 43), disability is ultimately an untranslatable sign and 'an unassimilable difference which threatens textual cohesion'. In terms of disability representation, Punter (2000: 40) sees the Gothic encounter with disability as 'a history of invasion and resistance, of the enemy within, of bodies torn and tortured, or else rendered miraculously, or sometimes catastrophically, whole'. Following Davis, Punter (2000: 41) reads Edward Hyde, in Robert Louis Stevenson's *Dr Jekyll and Mr Hyde* (1886), as functioning prosthetically, forming the 'overactive but inseparably disabled body' of Dr Jekyll, and thus destroying 'the fantasy of the wholly able body'. Punter (2000: 47) points to the future possibilities of developing readings that focus on 'disability and power', as 'the Gothic is, in any reading, about power'.

Theories of normalcy, deviance, and abjection prompt a considerable number of explorations of Gothic literature as emblematic of difference and deviance.[13] This is a major feature of the essays in Anolik's *Demons of the Body and Mind*.

---

[10] For early Disability Studies work on Gothic and the Romantic period, see Punter, 2000; Liggins, 2000; Gigante, 2000; Mossman, 2001; Purinton, 2001; Youngquist, 2003; Krentz, 2004.

[11] For early Disability Studies work Gothic and Victorian period, see Klages, 1999; Holmes, 2004; Schalk, 2008.

[12] For early Disability Studies work on Gothic across the nineteenth century, see Frawley, 2004; McDonagh, 2008; Mossman, 2009a; Mossman, 2009b.

[13] See, for example, Karschay, 2015; Kremmel, 2016; Tarr, 2017; Logan, 2019; Huff & Holmes, 2020.

In her introduction, Anolik (2010: 2) positions Gothic as a 'shadowy, mysterious and unknowable space inhabited by the inhumanly unknowable Other – supernatural or human'. There is complexity in this othering, as Anolik (2010: 2) observes: 'The Gothic presents human difference as monstrous, and then, paradoxically, subverts the categories of exclusion to argue for the humanity of the monster.' Gothic's resistance to 'limiting boundaries and defining categories' is, according to her, aligned 'with the disability rights movement' (Anolik, 2010: 5). While Gothic uses non-normative bodies to shock or scare, Anolik (2010: 6) also suggests that the reverse is possible: 'Gothic texts that categorize human disability as frighteningly inhuman deviance, tend conversely to interrogate cultural preoccupations with definition and categorization – in other words, with diagnosis.' Demons are characters 'who are diagnosed and the demonically powerful and even evil physicians who do the diagnosing' (Anolik, 2010: 6). Like Anolik, Costa (2019: 5) expresses concern about Gothic's negative potential, suggesting that 'representational traditions have long equated the disabled body with the monstrous body, metaphorically linking the qualities of monsters to the lived experience of disability or chronic illness'. Costa (2019: 6) concludes, however, that the Gothic is 'a space of possibility and peril'.

In the wake of the work of Mitchell and Snyder, and Tobin Siebers, prosthetic uses of disability and concepts of disability passing are a combined feature of several readings.[14] For instance, Kathleen Hudson (2018: 15, 17), writing in Costa's special issue, uses Siebers's work on disability masquerade to make the case that male characters in *The Monk*, such as Don Raymond, who fakes blindness, and Theodore, who adopts an eye patch, 'embrace a false "spoiled", Gothicized identity' that articulates 'a more general Gothic anxiety about identity performance'.[15] Jared S. Richman (2018: 191) also finds Siebers's ideas on passing generative. Richman suggests that for Frankenstein's creature, the acquisition of language is 'part of a strategy in which he attempts to construct his own identity in response to his perceived physical deformity', and that it constitutes an attempt at passing.

Several commentators note that Gothic literature often draws on Early Modern accounts of deformity and monstrosity, where deformity signals an omen, a punishment, or a wonder, and has a moral or religious significance.[16] Cynthia Hall (2010: 35) suggests, for instance, that 'misshapen corporeality' corresponds to an 'outward reflection of inner evil', and that this is 'a persistent trope for the disabled and the deformed'. Hall's reading of the American Gothic

---

[14] See, for example, Warne, 2005.   [15] See Siebers, 2004, 2008.
[16] See Deustch & Nussbaum, 2000.

novel *The Quaker City* (1845) hints at the 'recirculation' model of disability, where the use of deformity and defect as a signal of moral depravity in former ages is reiterated in the present.[17] Deformity's traditionally close connection with evil is, however, handled by nineteenth-century Gothic literature in complex ways. Tamara S. Wagner (2010: 47), for example, makes the case that Wilkie Collins 'shuttles between sympathetic accounts of deformity and warnings of the dangers of disability', and that Collins uses 'the deformed villain' as 'a false lead in detective plots' that play out through 'both sensational and Gothic clichés'.[18] She concludes that Count Fosco and Miserrimus Dexter suggest a 're-formation of the deformed, monstrous Gothic body (and mind)', and, like the monster figure, they interrogate 'the boundaries that conventionally and comfortably define the norm', and at the same time dismantle 'prejudices evoked to mislead and to surprise unsuspecting readers' (Wagner, 2010: 52, 51–2, 54). Gothic deformity's conventionality is, then, sometimes a deflector of expectations.[19] Deformed characters, however, are traditionally evil, and their deformities are sometimes identified as caused by supernatural means. Simon J. White, for example, notes the survival of folk-knowledge about deformity in Thomas Hardy's Gothic short story, 'The Withered Arm' (1888). For White (2010: 76), this 'story reveals an anxiety of the modern age: the fear of sliding back into dark superstition'.

Thomson's (and Foucault's) theories about sight-based stigma are important to Gothic Disability Studies. Paul Marchbanks (2010: 24) suggests that, in *Frankenstein* (1818) and *The Last Man* (1826), Mary Shelley 'creates a sustained dismantling of society's ocular and physiognomic apparatus', presenting 'visions of community that might welcome instead of expelling the disabled'.[20] Marchbanks (2010: 28–9) reads Shelley as 'contesting the idea that blindness is inferior to normative sight, suggesting advantages to blindness', and exploring the 'tantalizing glimpse[s] of disabled community' in her work. Visibility and invisibility are also important to Anolik's (2010: 10) account of Gothic disability, where she asserts that Gothic's 'impulse to render invisible difference as horrifying spectacle' and its 'tendency to make the invisible visible' is part of its 'irrational counter to the rational Enlightenment'. Anolik (2010: 10–11) finds in this counter-cultural propensity 'the Gothic movement toward liberation, exhibiting the realm of human experience that the Enlightenment attempts to repress'.

---

[17] For the recirculation model, see Joshua, 2020: 8–9.
[18] For more on Collins, sensation, and disability, see Mangum, 1998; Flint, 2006; Mossman & Holmes, 2011: 50; Esmail, 2013; Zigarovich, 2018: 99–111; Gore, 2020; Hingston, 2020; Tomaiuolo, 2022.
[19] See also Delyfer, 2010.   [20] See also Joshua, 2011, 2020: 155–80.

Given the distrust of medical authority in Disability Studies and the importance of Freud in Gothic Studies (particularly his theory of the uncanny), psychological readings of the Gothic pose a difficulty for Gothic Disability Studies. Gothic Studies has tended to take a diagnostic approach to Gothic madness and neurodiversity in ways that reinforce alterity, and centre diagnosis and medical perspectives. As the example from Davis earlier shows, however, Freudian and Lacanian readings are sometimes used in Disability Studies to explain some of the ways disabled characters are othered.[21] Martha Stoddard Holmes (2013: 182), for instance, suggests that, when the disabled body 'is used as a *source* or *object* of Gothic horror' it is often defamiliarized, in a Freudian sense (i.e., as something familiar that has been repressed and later returns in a different form). Cheyne (2019: 52, my italics) usefully separates 'texts that *feature* disability and produce "negative" feelings of fear and discomfort' from 'texts that *use* disability to produce feelings of fear and discomfort'. The latter, she demonstrates, 'might actually have positive *effects* in terms of shifting readers' perceptions of disability through the creation of reflexive representations' (Cheyne, 2019: 52). This reflexivity, she suggests, could take the form of the manipulation of stereotypes in ways that signal their lack of depth. For Cheyne (2019: 35), Gothic encourages 'readerly reflection on disability in a number of ways, from foregrounding disability-related prejudice to disrupting reductive images of disability'.

Esmail and Keep (2009: 47) point out that there are some reservations within Disability Studies over the extent to which Women's Studies and Gender Studies have embraced Disability Studies. They note that, while 'feminist scholars ... have expertly drawn attention to the social function' of the pathologizing of 'invalidism, hysteria, and madness', disability is often 'itself left undertheorized' or problematically reduced to 'a pitiable state of biological lack'. Nevertheless, these fields have been instrumental in laying some of the theoretical groundwork for Disability Studies, and there are a number of important critics and theorists who engage in both. Margrit Shildrick, in *Embodying the Monster*, for instance, observes that women and disabled people are treated as the monstrous binary other of the normative male. Shildrick (2000: 81) takes a postmodern deconstructionist approach to monstrosity, seeing it both as fulfilling 'the necessary function of the binary opposite that confirms the normality and centrality of the accultured self' and as threatening 'to disrupt that binary by being all too human'.

---

[21] For a recent revisionist psychoanalytic Disability Studies account of *Frankenstein*, see Wallace, 2020.

The re-appropriation of the madwoman has been an important strand in Feminist Disability Studies approaches to Gothic literature. We see the beginnings of this in the landmark work of second-wave Anglo-American feminist criticism, Sandra M. Gilbert and Susan Gubar's *The Madwoman in the Attic* (1984: 1979). This study uses madness as a metaphor to challenge Harold Bloom's *The Anxiety of Influence* (1973). Bloom's account of authorship, centred on anxiety-based intergenerational aggression and competition, omitted consideration of women writers. In their counter-narrative, Gilbert and Gubar (1984: 51) argued that women writers searched for female precursors who provided examples of the revolt against patriarchal literary authority. In doing so, women writers are handed down 'a germ of dis-ease', 'a disaffection, a disturbance, a distrust. that spreads like a stain throughout' their female subculture. 'Patriarchal socialization literally makes women sick, both physically and mentally', they suggest (Gilbert & Gubar, 1984: 53). Bertha Rochester's madness is read as a rebellion against patriarchal authority. Elizabeth J. Donaldson's (2002: 102) Disability Studies reading of *Jane Eyre*, however, rejects Gilbert and Gubar's idea of Bertha Rochester's madness as rebellion, arguing that 'when madness is used as a metaphor for feminist rebellions, mental illness is itself erased'. Donaldson's essay is reprinted in an important collection on *Jane Eyre*, the first Disability Studies revisionist book on a single text, *The Madwoman and the Blindman* (2012), edited by David Bolt, Julia Miele Rodas, and Elizabeth Donaldson.[22]

Scholars working in Queer Gothic Studies have also begun to engage more fully with Disability Studies approaches. Jason S. Farr's *Novel Bodies: Disability and Sexuality in Eighteenth-Century British Literature* (2019) makes the case for the importance of an intersectional minority understanding of disability. Farr offers a queer–crip reading of the seminal work of Gothic fiction, Horace Walpole's *The Castle of Otranto* (1764). Building on the work of disability–queer theorist Robert McRuer, Farr (2019: 16) reads the death of Conrad, the tyrannical Manfred's chronically ill son, as 'the queer, disabled catalyst of the plot, and by extension, of the early British gothic genre'. Conrad is queer in the sense that 'he stands outside of the normative frameworks of heterosexual desire and patrilineal succession due to his "sickly" constitution' (2019: 17).[23] For Farr (2019: 11), 'crip bodies contest the logic of heteronormativity'. Jeremy Chow (2023: 18) continues the conversation beyond Conrad to Hippolita in his discussion of 'the literary and material realms by which representations of deformity, womanhood and sexuality cohere in the

---

[22] Additional studies that investigate feminism, Gothic, and disability include: Miller, 2012; Aceves, 2018.
[23] See also Farr, 2020.

Romantic Gothic'. Chow (2023: 21) reads Hippolita's age-related 'sterility as an implicit semaphore of a deformed in/ability to participate in compulsory, reproductive heteronormativity'.

Ageing Studies shares much with Disability Studies as it is often characterized through impairments; and, as Zoe Brennan points out, old age is, like disability, underdiscussed in Gothic Studies. Avril Horner and Sue Zlosnik (2016: 184) devote brief attention to Ann Radcliffe and Charlotte Brontë in their discussion of 'the intersections between age and gender in the Gothic', observing that 'age-related hegemonic misogyny is either endorsed and reinforced or challenged in Gothic texts'. They find that 'older women are for the most part entirely dispensable' in Gothic fiction, appearing as abandoned wives, absent mothers, malicious childless women, or as wives and assistants to the evil patriarch (Horner & Zlosnik, 2016: 185). Roslyn Joy Irving (2022: 14) reminds us that ageing is as much 'a mental and physical process' as a gendered one. Frailty and ill health, she argues, makes aged characters liminal figures 'existing on the boundary of life and death' (Irving, 2022: 17). Irving (2022: 14) suggests a dialectical relationship between the ageing male body and the Radcliffian heroine who is 'poised between childhood and adulthood, forever in the act of becoming someone'. Ageing is a reminder of the temporarily able-bodied status of normate bodies, and as such it is frequently stigmatized in Gothic literature.

Medical Gothic is being re-examined in the light of Disability Studies, offering new conversations between Disability Studies and the Medical Humanities.[24] Writing within the field of the Medical Humanities, Sara Wasson (2015: 1) observes that 'Gothic literature and film has long had an interest in the way medical practice controls, classifies and torments the body in the service of healing'. Where the critical emphasis is on patient perspective and experience, and on what Wasson (2015: 7) calls 'medicine gone wrong', the Medical Humanities shares ground with Disability Studies. Like Disability Studies scholars, Wasson (2015: 7) sees 'cultural studies of medicine' as 'analysing representations of the way medical discourses, medical practices and globalised biotechnological networks can, at times, do (inadvertent) violence to human bodies and minds – both of patient and practitioner'. Importantly, it is the Gothic dimension of the texts that makes them align with a distrust of medicine. As Wasson (2015: 8) puts it, 'Gothic studies of medicine will inevitably explore the shadow side'. We see some further connections between the two fields in another essay by Wasson (2020: 75), in which she finds value in the idiosyncratic use of 'disjointed temporalities' in Gothic,

---

[24] See Wang, 2011; Holmes, 2018; Lau, 2019; Sweet, 2022.

where, for example, a ghost from one century visits another. This, she comments, shares some consonance with 'crip time', where disabled people recognize that time units are used in normative ways, and how long things take means different things to different people.[25]

Concepts of illness and concepts of disability are not easily distinguishable, and examining such distinctions historically means taking into account the differences in the definition of disability and in the state of medical knowledge. Of the new directions in which Disability Studies is developing in relation to illness, care ethics is one of the most recent. Care has traditionally been talked about within Disability Studies as belonging to a 'medical model' approach to disability that is antithetical to its principles. Traditionally the medical professions focus on returning patients to 'normal', and preserve a hierarchical separation of the helper and the helped. Talia Schaffer and D. Christopher Gabbard, however, articulate how readings that incorporate care ethics in ways sensitive to patient dignity build on ideas about interdependence that are already important to Disability Studies.[26] Disability Studies is distinct from the Medical Humanities as it does not centre medical treatments, diagnosis, medical science, or medical concerns; and some disabilities may not need medical care.[27] To some extent Care Studies bridges the gap between these fields. Care Studies also returns to concepts of the vulnerability and the materiality of the body that were present early in Disability Studies.

Disability Studies has moved on from negative image approaches, but Gothic subject matter requires some sensitivity, given that the genre is one of extremes. This may go some way to explaining why Disability Studies has yet to fully embrace the Gothic. Critics are understandably concerned that this subject matter is engaged with responsibly. Wasson (2020: 70) reminds us that 'representations of disability in Gothic literature have most often been toxic, limiting, and corrosive'. She cautions, further, that 'in its relentless interest in fear and distress, Gothic seems diametrically opposed to the important political goal of countering negative representations of disability' (Wasson, 2020: 71). Wasson (2020: 70) identifies three aspects of Gothic negativity for closer attention: 'a preoccupation with protagonists enduring misery and isolation; traditions of depicting unconventional bodies and minds in terms of monstrosity; and the way the mode lends itself to a narrative of an individual fallen into misfortune'. She, nevertheless, makes the case that there is value in examining disability in the Gothic mode. We might, she suggests, use Gothic to balance the emphasis

---

[25] For more on "crip time," see Kafer, 2013. [26] See also Holmes, 2007.

[27] For a sample of Gothic Medical Humanities, see: Roche, 2009; Hughes, 2012; Starkowski, 2017; Kremmel, 2022; Reznicek, 2023. See also *Gothic Studies* 17:1 (2015) for a special issue on Medical Gothic.

on positivity in recent Disability Studies accounts of literature: 'Gothic's preoccupation with distress can itself be a useful counter to forms of positivity that can lead to excluding some people's experience of disability and chronic illness' (Wasson, 2020: 74). It can also 'be effective in communicating social injustice' (Wasson, 2020: 75).

Much of the recent critical attention to disability and the Gothic has focused on finding moments of empowerment, where deviance is embraced or becomes an advantage, and stigmatizers are denounced. The goal for many critics engaged in Gothic Disability Studies has recently been the rehabilitation of the genre. Holmes (2013: 182) recognizes that, since Anolik's book, 'there have been only isolated explorations of the role of disability in fictions and films that can be classified as Gothic or as containing Gothic elements', and provides insight into the wide range of approaches to disability in Gothic literature we might take. She finds that, although 'the preponderance of representations of disability in the Gothic mode' may well 'objectify it, using the gothicization of disability as way to process a horror of people with disabilities (with the result of promulgating such a horror), there are significant exceptions to this pattern', such as *Frankenstein* and *Dracula*. (Holmes, 2013: 183). Holmes (2013: 184) sensibly decides that 'there is no one mode of "Gothic disability"', a feature she finds makes it 'a rich topic', and, furthermore, observes that 'there is promise for much more work in the realm of theorizing Gothic disability, simply by considering various theoretical modes already linked to the Gothic – abjection, the excessive Rabelaisian body (Bahktin), queer Gothic, and Gothic pathology, to note the most obvious – as critical concepts that can be productively repurposed as "about" disability as a cultural construct'.

There are a number of strategies used in Gothic Disability Studies to demonstrate how Gothic literature can be critically repositioned away from its problematic use of disability as a source of fear. For example, the dehumanization of disabled characters is a concern for many critics of Gothic literature, but often critics find subtlety amidst this ableism. Fuson Wang (2017: 7; 2) observes, for instance, that recovering Gothic literature has been delayed because of what he calls 'ungenerous reading' that politicized an 'ableist past' with 'an urgent politics of anachronistic resentment' instead of historicizing the reading of disability. For Wang (2017: 3), *Frankenstein* in particular has been caught up in a transhistorical appropriation of disability that he aims to correct by reconstructing 'a cultural climate of disability'.[28] Wang (2017: 7) argues that the novel's association with making disabled people seem monstrous meant that 'to

---

[28] Wang asserts that 'there still exists no detailed account of its [*Frankenstein*'s] take on disability' (p. 3). Several Disability Studies readings of *Frankenstein* do predate his article, however. See Gigante, 2000; Krentz, 2004; Lacom, 2005; Joshua, 2011; Rodas, 2016.

recover *Frankenstein* for disability studies is a steep uphill battle'. From the early 2000s, however, we see a shift in the attention to ableism in Gothic from the accusatory to the nuanced. Christopher Krentz (2004: 200) urges, for instance, that *Frankenstein* could be reclaimed as a symbol of empowerment, as it shows 'the importance of taking pride in who we are, of embracing difference and disability'. In her article on Edith Nesbit's late nineteenth-century Gothic short stories, Kathleen A. Miller (2012: 144) argues that 'the depiction of disability may serve an empowering political function' that expresses a feminist agenda. Miller (2012: 144) suggests that 'disability creates an opportunity for transcendence of the unequal, exploitative, and, at times, abusive gendered binaries deployed in other forms of traditional romance rhetoric'.

While space does not permit a full survey, the two sections that follow will consider texts from the early, mid, and late nineteenth century, to provide a sense of the range within two key topics: Gothic bodies, and Gothic minds (madness and neurodiversity). I acknowledge that the nineteenth century does not entirely separate bodies and minds, and so this division is to some extent artificial. Madness, for instance, is understood physiologically as well as behaviourally in this period.[29] The section on Disability and the Gothic Body will focus on the many ways in which Gothic texts reveal deep-seated fears about the human body, and how writers sometimes question the injustice of treating bodily difference as something terrifying. Much of this discussion will point to the different ways of looking at visibly anomalous characters in the Gothic, and to the different affective responses to disability. Each text discussed in this section will illustrate a different mode in which Gothic bodies articulate and shift their relationship to aesthetic and affective frameworks. Melancholy, mania, and neurasthenia (or hysteria) are the three most popular nineteenth-century mad diagnoses, though there is overlap between them and a great deal of flexibility about how they are defined. Section 3 discusses diagnostic uncertainties as well as the different roles that mad and neurodivergent characters perform in Gothic narratives. The focus here is on Gothic approaches to understanding alternative ways of being in the world, as well as on important tropes: madness outside is different from madness indoors, for instance. Like the Gothic castle, the asylum is a space where power governs the vulnerable. Gothic links pursuit to paranoia, and despair is attached to multiple types of madness. In the discussion that follows, the literary texts will be discussed chronologically, but the discussions are intended to build on

---

[29] For important early work on madness, see Foucault 1965; Showalter 1985; Porter 1987; Faas 1988; Ingram 1991; Small 1996.

each other in ways that introduce a range of Disability Studies theoretical approaches incrementally.

2 Disability and the Gothic Body

We begin with an examination of John Keats's *Lamia* (1820) as a vehicle for anxieties about monstrous bodies. These anxieties illustrate Lennard Davis's account of the Venus–Medusa binary. Lamia briefly acquires a beautiful body that masks her snake–woman hybridity until a non-consensual revelation forces a direct engagement with the illusory quality of the normate body. Next, Elizabeth Gaskell's 'The Well of Pen-Morfa' (1850) explores disability embodiment in the context of networks of care. Here there is a reciprocity of care relationships between a woman who is physically disabled and one who is intellectually disabled. H. Rider Haggard's *She* (1887) disrupts implied able-bodied norms of what David Mitchell and Sharon Snyder (2015: 45) call 'capacitated citizenship' while pursuing a eugenicist and imperialist agenda. Disability and deformity are used here to partially displace an expected narrative of White heroism, ideals of White beauty, and able-bodied hierarchies, in favour of interracial cooperation, White deformity, physical dependency, and care. Ultimately, the novel renegotiates the value of the latter features, revising our sense of disability and capacitated citizenship whilst maintaining an imperialist racial hierarchy. Thomas Hardy's short story 'The Withered Arm' (1888) follows the emotional journey of a farmer's beautiful young wife whose arm is disabled by the curse of her husband's former lover, the mother of his child. Hardy explores the difficulties of acquiring a stigmatized attribute – paralleling the experience of the fallen woman with that of the disabled woman – and the ways in which both women negotiate reputational and disability stigmas. In the final section, W. W. Jacobs, in 'Three At Table' (1899), describes how a man with facial burns, and his family, manage the potentially negative reactions to his appearance by pretending that his eyes need a dark environment. The story draws attention to stigma by experimenting with disability passing. Jacobs concludes the story by offering a moment of acceptance, and an admission that the context in which Gothicized disability is encountered can heighten a sense of fear.

These five texts cohere around three areas of interest for scholars interested in disability and the body. Firstly, all of the texts are concerned with how non-normative bodies are subjected to sight-based stigma. Secondly, *Lamia*, 'The Well of Pen-Morfa', and 'Three at Table' also explore the problem of an individual's body autonomy; and, finally, *Lamia*, 'The Well of Pen-Morfa', *She*, and 'The Withered Arm' address questions around disability's relationship to community.

2.1 Uncanny Bodies in John Keats's *Lamia* (1820)

In his 1919 essay 'Das Unheimliche', Freud defines the uncanny as a hidden or taboo thing that is revealed or unveiled. The uncanny provokes an emotional response to a familiar thing that has become alienated through the process of repression. We see the uncanny in many features of Gothic literature, such as dolls, doubles, repetitions, mummies, mirrors, secrets, severed limbs, automata, and the reanimation of the dead. Drawing on Freud and Lacan, the disability theorist Lennard Davis (1995: 132) argues that the disabled body is an uncanny reminder of the illusion of wholeness, a reminder that brings to the surface a repressed sense of the self as a fragmented body. Medusa is a Gothic uncanny figure who 'is the necessary counter [to Venus] in the dialectic of beauty and ugliness, desire and repulsion, wholeness and fragmentation'.

Keats's 'Lamia' is a Gothic neoclassical poem set in Crete and Corinth. In part one, the god Hermes falls in love with a nymph who has hidden herself from him. While searching for her, he hears the voice of a beautiful female snake, Lamia, who wants to return to her former fully human state and 'move in a sweet body fit for life' (Keats, 1982: 343 [I.39]). Lamia as snake has a hybrid body: her snake torso is multi-coloured and she has a woman's mouth, eyes, and teeth. In return for Hermes helping her regain her female body, Lamia removes the power of invisibility that she has given to the nymph.

The extended scene describing Lamia's metamorphosis from hybrid snake–woman to woman engages in what Davis calls the dialectic of attraction and repulsion. We follow her fragmented ego's painful transformation into the illusion of the whole, 'a full-born beauty new and exquisite' (Keats, 1982: 346 [I.172]). Although he does not discuss Lamia, Davis's characterization of the interplay between the normative and the disabled as a Venus–Medusa binary resonates with Keats's poem. For Davis (1995: 132), the snake-like 'Medusa is a poignant double' for Venus. Medusa 'is the necessary counter in the dialectic of beauty and ugliness, desire and repulsion, wholeness and fragmentation' (Davis, 1995: 132). Lamia's adopted body highlights the constructedness and instability of the desired normate body.

In developing his theory of the uncanny, Davis reinterprets the Lacanian mirror phase, where a child recognizes itself as separate from the mother, as a misrecognition. In her mirror phase, Lamia looks in 'a clear pool, wherein she passioned / To see herself escap'd from so sore ills' (Keats, 1982: 346 [II.183–4]). Lamia's new body is her ego's armour against the chaotic and fragmented body. In her acquired illusory body, Lamia intends to woo Lycius, 'a youth of Corinth', who immediately falls in love with her (Keats, 1982: 344 [II.119]). She takes him to her magnificent mansion, built and serviced by magic, where they live a luxurious though secluded life. The home is in the heart of Corinth, yet it is unfamiliar (*unheimlich*) and unfindable by the inhabitants: 'the most curious / were foil'd, who watch'd to trace' their servants 'to their house' (Keats, 1982: 351 [II.391–3]). In part two of the poem, after Lamia has accepted Lycius's proposal of marriage, the wedding guests find the house *unheimlich*, too, each 'marveling: for they knew the street, / Remember'd it from childhood all complete / Without a gap, yet ne'er before had seen / That royal porch, that high-built fair demesne' (Keats, 1982: 355 [II.152–5]).

Lamia accepts the proposal, provided Lycius's philosopher mentor, Apollonius, is not invited to the wedding. When Apollonius nevertheless attends the wedding, he looks at Lamia with 'with eye severe', and, his 'philosophy' or scientific knowledge has the ability to 'clip an Angel's wings' and 'Unweave a rainbow' (Keats, 1982: 355, 357, 357 [II.157; 234; 237]). With a fixed stare, Apollonius cries out to Lamia '"Begone, foul dream!"' (Keats, 1982: 358 [II.271]). Lycius, troubled by Apollonius's penetrating gaze, a staple of Gothic fiction, asks the gods to blind his mentor, denouncing his 'demon eyes' (Keats, 1982: 358 [II.289]). The physicality of Apollonius's gaze makes it tactile: 'the sophist's eye, / Like a sharp spear, went through her utterly, cruel, perceant, stinging' (Keats, 1982: 358 [II.299–301]). As Davis (1995: 147) observes, 'the specular moment leads to the tactile moment'. Lamia's skin, a marker of her fragmented ego, becomes 'deadly white' and, 'no longer fair' (Keats, 1982: 358 [II.276]). She vanishes at the point Apollonius calls her a serpent, and Lycius instantly dies. Lamia's *unheimlich* home disappears with her body.

Lamia's story resonates with Davis's account of the normate reaction to the disabled body, as a moment of insight where the normate recognizes their own body as incomplete. Lamia's body is a prosthesis that fits with the world's beauty standards. The revelation of her snake body is forced by Apollonius's rationalist gaze, a gaze that Lycius fights with his prayer that the gods phallically pierce his eyes 'with the thorn of sudden blindness' (Keats, 1982: 358 [II.281]). Lycius is, however, left with neither the normate (beautiful woman) nor the fragmented body (the snake) and dies moments after Lamia's disappearance. The dual disappearance of woman and snake reinforces the connectedness of the Venus–Medusa binary, and Lycius's death emphasizes his love for Lamia. While uncanny bodies are often thought of as threatening, and are responded to with fear and anxiety, Lamia's closeted body is outed against her wishes, raising our sympathies and prompting us to think about her privacy. She leaves before she is shamed, however, and her disappearance adumbrates her power in absenting herself from the stigmatizing gaze. Nevertheless, Lamia's exposure is double-edged: it rehearses her own revelation of the invisible nymph who hid from Hermes's lust, and may well hint at a punishment for her earlier removal of the nymph's protection.

Davis's approach demonstrates how psychoanalytical theorizing of the Gothic body in Disability Studies differs from more conventional pathologizing studies that deem the disabled body problematic, or emblematic of non-normative psychology. 'Lamia' plays with the notion of the illusoriness of a wholeness that is common to all humans, and is a vehicle for anxieties about disability closeting. Non-consensual revelations of bodily difference and sight-based stigma are adverted to numerous times in Gothic literature, and we shall return to this at the end of the section, in a discussion of W. W. Jacobs's 'Three At Table'. The disconnectedness of Lamia from a community, while it mimics the marginalization of disabled people, stands in contrast to the Victorian narratives of care we shall look at next.

2.2 Communities of Care in Elizabeth Gaskell's 'The Well of Pen-Morfa' (1850)

The politics of care has become an important part of the discussion of disability. Traditionally avoided because of its association with the medicalization of disability, and because disability has too often been assumed to be inseparable from medical issues, care is now recognized as an important part of the history of all people. Care relationships and acts of care are significant because they give us an idea of the cultures around disability. Care – whether formal, through professional caregivers and institutions, or found in more informal situations, such as companions or relatives caring for each other in domestic spaces – has, along with its corollaries, abuse and neglect, been central to the social and domestic understanding of disability. Care appears in nineteenth-century Gothic literature in many ways, but it is most visible in institutions such as asylums (see Section 3). In the Gothic mode, institutions of care are often mechanisms for the powerful to persecute the vulnerable. Nevertheless, characters can challenge and survive threats in Gothic texts through intervention from people in caregiving roles, as well as through their own agency and self-advocacy. Gothic literature presents care relationships both as creating horror and as resolving it.

In her work on ethical approaches to reading informed by Disability Studies, Talia Schaffer (2021: 7) distinguishes care *actions* from care *feelings* to maintain a sense of the care professions as occupations, and to signal an 'expanded idea of character' in which a character's care 'acts do not necessarily reveal a deeper self' or presuppose care feelings. As Schaffer (2021: 5; 35) observes, 'care is an action, not a feeling', and it can be defined simply as 'meeting another's needs'. A 'good care dynamic', Schaffer (2021: 10) asserts, occurs when 'the roles of carer and cared-for constantly switch' and there is good communication. Moreover, caring describes a positionality. One is either cared for or one cares. Nevertheless, these positions are, Schaffer (2021: 6) claims, fluid and discursive.

In her account of the structural qualities of care communities, Schaffer (2021: 49) counts five distinct, but interconnected, features that characterize them, but that work differently in different types of care community: 'performativity, discursivity, affiliation, egalitarianism, and temporality'. The effects of caregiving and receiving on an individual's sense of self are important for well-being, according to Schaffer. Importantly for Gothic literature, communities of care may sustain their sociability even across the divide between the living and the dead. As Schaffer goes on to show, caregivers in a broader sense may include animals, the wider natural world, or books.

Different aspects of care are sometimes more visible than others and it may be that the polite aspects of caring (sitting at a bedside) are more apparent than the actions of someone who 'empties bedpans and wipes up vomit' (Schaffer, 2021: 14–15). Furthermore, care communities may describe support structures for those for whom traditional family units are not possible (e.g., 'queer families of choice'), or for indigenous communities; and they may suggest undervalued feminized or maternal practices. Care relationality places the discussion of disability into a broader social framework where 'disability simply becomes a point on a spectrum of need, evoking a response just like any other need' (Schaffer, 2021: 36). Schaffer concludes that the mid nineteenth century is pivotal in the movement towards medicalized ideas about suffering that were different from the idea of suffering as a natural part of the human condition. Medicalized approaches to suffering, she argues, tended to be more dramatic, where heroic interventions by experts characterized accounts of responses to illness. In her short story 'The Well of Pen-Morfa', Elizabeth Gaskell writes in the mould of this mid-century paradigm, but steers away from the medical model of expert intervention by engaging with the idea of disabled families of choice (i.e., families one is not born into).[30]

The story addresses questions arising from *affiliation* in communities of care. Schaffer (2021: 47) defines 'affiliation' as 'the notion that carers join the care community voluntarily' and 'is the idea behind the Victorian dream of ideal women's angelic love of nursing'. Gaskell, moreover, incorporates a quasi-fallen woman story, and the care community that develops involves the dead. Martha Stoddard Holmes (2002: 30, 36) offers a reading of this story that

---

[30] The story was first published in Dickens's *Household Words* on 23 November 1850, and later in *Lizzie Leigh; and Other Tales* (London: Chapman and Hall, 1865), with a further edition in the same year published by Smith and Elder.

concentrates on 'interdependence' as a 'norm', arguing that interdependence is most commonly present in Victorian fiction as 'two characters in a caring relationship characterized by an emotional parity that subsumes their symmetry as physical or social agents' (i.e., their relationship is more important than their social status or physical attributes). In 'The Well of Pen-Morfa', the 'dyads of care', as Holmes terms them, are firstly the mother–daughter relationship of Eleanor Gwynn and Nest, her beautiful 'fairy-gifted child', and, secondly, the relationship that develops at the end of the narrative between Nest and Mary Williams, who is described as a 'half-witted woman' (Gaskell, 1995: 126, 139). I would like to suggest, further, that these dyads are developed among affiliations to wider communities of care and amidst the idiosyncratic structure of this particular community.

The story is set in a real village in north-west Wales, a place that Gaskell associated with the illness of her daughter Marianne, who caught scarlet fever there in July 1845, and with her son, Willie, who died of the illness at Porthmadog, near Pen-Morfa. The first inclination of the idiosyncrasies of affiliation at Pen-Morfa are hinted at in the Welsh use of patronymics: 'the eldest son's name is John Jones, because his father's was John Thomas; ... the second son is called David Williams, because his grandfather was William Wynn; and ... the girls are called indiscriminately by the names of Thomas and Jones' (Gaskell, 1995: 123). These signals of social relationality bind generations in ways that are confusing to outsiders.

The narrator, who does a great deal of set-up work in the frame, is an English visitor interpreting the culture for other outsiders. This involves her taking a tour of the village, accompanied by a friend who speaks English and Welsh, to see the 'old primitive dwellings' (Gaskell, 1995: 125). The first house has 'an old couple' who share their 'milk and oatcake with patriarchal hospitality'; the husband is 'blind, or nearly so, and they sat one on each side of the fire, so old and so still (till we went in and broke the silence) that they seemed to be listening for death' (Gaskell, 1995: 125). The second house contains a 'severe-looking' beekeeper, living alone with her bees, who talks in a 'mournful tone' (Gaskell, 1995: 124). This house has been home to a disabled/non-disabled dyad, a mother and child. The woman had left domestic service pregnant and now lived by selling honey. When she gave birth, 'her child was deformed, and had lost the use of its lower limbs' (Gaskell, 1995: 125). The woman is described as spending years as a 'watching mother, solitary and friendless, soothing the moaning child' (Gaskell, 1995: 125). The beekeeper is well-respected, but prefers to care for her child alone: 'Her sorrow was so dignified, and her mute endurance and her patient love won her such respect, that the neighbours would fain have been friends; but she kept alone and solitary'

(Gaskell, 1995: 125). The patronymics that dissociate children from their parents' last names, the silent co-dependent old couple, and the woman who could be helped by her community but prefers to care alone, offer three distinct types of idiosyncratic affiliation that point to the subject matter that is to follow.

The story of the well, however, is older than these tales, and is one that belongs to the place rather than to the individuals the narrator directly encounters. It begins with the dyad of a widow, Eleanor Gwynn, and her daughter, Nest, a coquette. Nest's household task, a care action, is to fetch water from the well. Here she meets Edward Williams, a young farmer, and agrees to marry him. On a trip to the well, dressed in her best clothes and intending to meet Edward, Nest slips and falls. The story hints that her vanity and unchaperoned behaviour may be morally compromising, and so this may be a fall in the sense of a sexual indiscretion. Nest is immobilized for months in bed, and her mother watches over her 'with tenderest care'; the 'neighbours would come and offer help', bringing 'presents of country dainties', but Eleanor will not 'delegate the duty of watching over her child' (Gaskell, 1995: 129). Edward, however, is not a willing care-giver and abandons Nest. Her mother realizes he is not the 'protector' she had hoped for (Gaskell, 1995: 127). By way of an excuse, Edward tells Eleanor what the doctor has kept from her, that Nest will 'be a cripple for life' (Gaskell, 1995: 131). He claims that as a farmer, he needs an able-bodied wife. Eleanor selflessly offers to do the work, but Edward says that Nest ought to seek the hand of Mr Griffiths, who is wealthy enough to own a carriage that could assist with her mobility. Eleanor curses Edward, but promises him she will to try to lift the curse if he visits and pretends to care about Nest. As Nest's health improves, and she is able to walk with the assistance of a crutch, Edward's visits tail off, nevertheless, and Eleanor is obliged to tell Nest the truth: 'that her disabled frame was a disqualification for ever becoming a farmer's wife' (Gaskell, 1995: 134). Edward underestimates Nest, who is able to do 'hard work' and craves 'bodily fatigue', though not the company of her community (Gaskell, 1995: 134). Nest's grief is unresolved, and it comes to a head when Eleanor brings a neighbour's baby home to cheer Nest up; but Nest is troubled by not herself having the opportunity for this caring relationship: 'I shall never have a child to lie in my breast, and call me mother!' (Gaskell, 1995: 135). The mother and daughter go through a difficult period when Edward marries someone else, but they reconcile before Eleanor's death.

The loss of her mother makes Nest feel alone, and the Methodist minister, David Hughes, who comforted Eleanor in her final days, offers advice. Nest wishes her mother to 'come back as a spirit or a ghost' (Gaskell, 1995: 138). David offers another model for care, instead: 'you must love like Christ, without thought of self, or wish for return' (Gaskell, 1995: 138). In response to this call, Nest takes in Mary Williams, an intellectually disabled neighbour, to give her refuge from the violent household in which Mary has been forced to live. Eleanor had in the past given Mary food and comfort when she periodically ran away due to her brutal treatment, and so this relationship develops in the context of Nest's idea of maternal care. David accidentally witnesses a striking moment of tenderness, where Nest calms Mary, who is in distress, by talking softly to her and embracing her. The three pray together 'as if it were a charm to scare away the Demonic possession' (Gaskell, 1995: 140). Shortly after this, David, who is eighty-one, dies. Nest, whose melancholy has been cured by her care for Mary, ministers more widely to her community again, but her dyadic pairing with Mary is paramount: 'there were times when Mary was overpowered by the glooms and fancies of her poor disordered brain. ... On those days, Nest warned the little children who loved to come and play around her, that they must not visit the house', and 'the sorrowful and the sick waited in vain for the sound of Nest's lame approach' (Gaskell, 1995: 141). As Nest ages prematurely, the Gothic and melodramatic elements of the tale increase: a childhood scar on her hand begins to hurt; she begins to hear 'the cackling sound of the treacherous, rending wood'; and her mother's spirit visits her to bind her wound, extending her care relationship beyond the grave (Gaskell, 1995: 141).

Care reciprocity is important in Schaffer's account of care communities. Mary's and Nest's care dyad is generally depicted as a reciprocal one; there are, nevertheless, some problematic moments. The narrator suggests, for instance, that Mary returned Nest's love 'as a dumb animal loves its blind master' (Gaskell, 1995: 141). Mary demonstrates the reciprocity of the care relationship, however, by helping Nest to go back to the 'fatal well' she has not visited in the thirty years since her accident (Gaskell, 1995: 142). Nest preternaturally knows she is dying. In the night before the visit to the well, Nest's mother appears in her dream, 'not in the flesh, but in the bright glory of a blessed spirit' (Gaskell, 1995: 142). Nest dies as she leans against a rock, finding 'immortality by the well-side, instead of her fragile, perishing youth' (Gaskell, 1995: 142). Mary is sent to the workhouse, where she is occasionally soothed by tales of Nest. Through these stories, Nest's care for Mary, like Eleanor's for Nest, reaches beyond the grave. Nest and Mary become part of the folklore of the well.

'The Well of Pen-Morfa' illustrates a range of care relationships that are dynamic and reciprocal. For Mary and Nest, the roles of carer and cared-for are fluid. Gaskell moves beyond normative bonds to include disabled communities of care that enable inclusion of the intellectually disabled and marginalized

Mary. Schaffer's comment on the mid-century intervention of the expert response to the 'catastrophic event' is pertinent here, too, though it is handled with some complexity by Gaskell. The doctor is peripheral, and his true diagnosis of Nest's condition is received by her mother second hand. His role is superseded by the other 'expert' who intervenes, the preacher, who is crucial for Nest's emotional rehabilitation. But it is the relationship between Mary and Nest that is most important. Gaskell's story offers a range of communities of care, many of which are not ideal; but it demonstrates a strong interest in deep affiliations in disabled families of choice.

2.3 Gothic Biopower in H. Rider Haggard's *She* (1887)

Physical disability appears in H. Rider Haggard's novel *She* (1887) in multiple ways. It is at the heart of the novel's engagement with a range of approaches to Gothic power. Disability's presence in a colonialist narrative is unsurprising, given that anthropological accounts of racial hierarchies frequently make judgments about intellectual and physical capacities; but the questioning of able-bodied hierarchies, even as characters are tempted to seek super-abilities, is striking.

In *The Biopolitics of Disability*, the Disability Studies theorists David Mitchell and Sharon Snyder (2015: 18–19) examine some of the 'changes in cultural approaches to disability [that] have come about under neoliberalism', where disability is an 'exceptional status . . . based upon embodiments that are the responsibility of the individual and no fault of the social order'. They argue that there emerged at the end of the eighteenth century a conflation of ableism (the privileging of able-bodied and able-minded norms) and nationalism. Mitchell and Snyder combine this to form the term 'ablenationalism'. This they define as the treatment of people with disabilities 'as exceptional bodies in ways that further valorize able-bodied norms as universally desirable and as the . . . qualifications of fully capacitated citizenship to which others inevitably aspire' (Mitchell & Snyder, 2015: 44–5).

As a counter to this, Mitchell and Snyder (2015: 5) argue for what they term 'nonnormative positivism'. This is an 'alternative ethics of living': a way to learn from disabled people that our expectations should be flexible. Mitchell and Snyder (2015: 6) invite us to question our 'internalized scripts of embodied normativity'. Disability becomes, on this understanding, disruptive: not in the sense of deviant, but in the sense of re-orienting away from 'narrowly devised norms of capacity, functionality, and bodily aesthetic' (Mitchell & Snyder, 2015: 12). Mitchell and Snyder (2015: 6) call 'for an alternative ethics to be articulated about why disabled lives matter and how we might revise, reinvent, and transform narrow normative practices, beliefs, and qualifications of who counts'. Their work is influenced by Foucault's theory of biopower, which asserts that bodies and minds are caught up in systems of control through normalization and discipline.

In *She*, non-normative positivism (being flexible about expectations) challenges the ablenationalist assumptions that the novel sets up with its colonial outlook. Leo Vincey, the novel's hero, is presented as the aesthetic perfection of White manhood and the epitome of the Greek racial ideal. He is compared to a 'statue of Apollo' (Haggard, 2006: 52). Ayesha is a beautiful White Greek woman, a sorceress-like and snake-like figure who has conquered a territory in Africa and has claimed the position of queen through her ability to manipulate nature in an arcane way that appears magical. This knowledge, like the secrets in many Gothic texts, is dangerous and forbidden. Leo is the physical and spiritual reincarnation of her dead lover, and the goal of the plot is to reunite them. Leo's guardian Horace Holly, a Cambridge don, however, is described as 'branded like Cain' with 'the stamp of abnormal ugliness', though compensated with 'abnormal strength and considerable intellectual powers' (Haggard, 2006: 40). While Holly's deformity makes him a problematic symbol of Englishness, Leo's status as a racial paragon is also questioned. He is incapacitated by illness for much of the quest into Africa. Indeed, the quest to find Ayesha in the depths of Africa, with its Gothic-like ruined cities and mysterious and occasionally anthropomorphic landscapes, becomes a quest to cure him. Disabling the hero in a quest narrative unsettles the usual depiction of colonial strength, displacing an expected narrative of dominance and heroism with one of vulnerability, dependency, care, and cooperation.

The novel disrupts expectations about disability in other ways, too. The peoples that Ayesha controls are organized as a matriarchy, where women are physically weaker than, but socially superior to, men. Ayesha purposefully engages in eugenicist breeding. She does not produce a race without disability, however, but a guard of deaf women to protect her. They are, she says, 'the safest of servants ... I bred them so – it hath taken many centuries and much trouble; but at last I have succeeded' (Haggard, 2006: 152). The novel acknowledges that disability can be valued in the right contexts.

Charles Darwin's ideas were adapted many times in Gothic literature to promote anthropological ideas about racial difference, racial hierarchies, and sexual selection that had been emerging in scientific research since the eighteenth century. Darwin (1871: 1.171) remarks, for instance, that the ancient Greeks 'stood some grades higher in intellect than any race that has ever existed'. Aside from race, these ideas were also important for cultural responses to disability and deformity. Darwin (1871: 1.162) observes, for example, that 'vaccination has preserved thousands, who from a weak constitution would formerly have succumbed to small-pox', causing 'the weak members of civilized societies [to] propagate their kind'. He finds it incomprehensible that 'civilized nations' act in ways that are unnatural: 'With savages, the weak in body or mind are soon eliminated' (Darwin, 1871: 1.161). So-called civilized nations, however, 'build asylums for the imbecile, the maimed, and the sick; we institute poor-laws; and our medical men exert their utmost skill to save the life of every one to the last moment' (Darwin, 1871: 1.161–2). Darwin's writing on the shared ancestry of humans and apes is also significant. In *She*, Haggard blurs the distinctions between human and non-human animals to recognize the unstable boundaries of a post-Darwinian world. Holly is given the nickname 'Baboon', Leo is the lion, Billali is 'Billy-goat', and Job is 'the Pig on account of his fatness, round face, and small eyes' (Haggard, 2006: 114;115;125). There is even a direct reference to Darwin. A woman comments at the beginning of the novel that Holly's appearance makes her sympathetic to Darwin's (1871: 2.361) idea in *The Descent of Man* (1871) that humans and apes shared a common ancestor: 'Man, as I have attempted to show, is certainly descended from some ape-like creature'. Ayesha, famously, reverts to a monkey at her demise, when she re-enters the flame that she expects to give her immortality. Like Victor Frankenstein, she symbolizes science's ability to go beyond the limitations of the human condition; but the novel also offers a counterpoint that questions the value placed on able and beautiful White bodies and their ablenationalist implications. While the novel calls into question perfectibility as a species goal, and the use of physical strength as a determiner of hierarchy, it leaves intact imperialist assumptions about racial hierarchies and the stigmatized attributes of racialized bodies. *She* suggests that Gothic bodies engage in a biopolitical defamiliarization rather than normalisation, and that this defamiliarization destabilizes disability, gender, and racial hierarchies.

2.4 Stigmatized Bodies: Thomas Hardy's 'The Withered Arm' (1888)

Erving Goffman's sociological studies on the processes that govern stigma have been important in the development of the foundational theories in Disability Studies. Beginning with the idea that a person has a social category and personal attributes that make up their social identity, Goffman explains that this social identity generates normative expectations about them. These normative expectations are their *virtual social identity*. Goffman posits that this is separate from their *actual social identity*, which is their real status. A stigma is a socially determined value placed on an attribute that deviates from social expectations.

A person with a stigma has 'a special discrepancy between virtual and actual social identity' (Goffman, 1986: 3). Goffman suggests that the language of relationality is preferred because the attribute might have different meanings in different contexts. He calls people who do not have a discrepancy in their relationship to expectations, 'normals'. Normals treat the stigmatized as not quite human or act on false notions about disability, such as talking loudly to blind people. 'Mixed contacts' are 'moments when normal and the stigmatized are in the same social situation' in what Goffman calls 'anxious and unanchored interaction[s]' (Goffman, 1986: 12, 18). These are uneasy and self-conscious moments where a lot of unacknowledged mental processing goes on, such as avoiding taboo words or asking unusually intimate questions.

Thomas Hardy's short story 'The Withered Arm' was first published in *Blackwood's Magazine* (January 1888), and was later published in *Wessex Tales*, a collection devoted to a semi-fictional region of England that stretched from the Thames in the east to Devon. Hardy's aim in this volume is to record, romanticize, and sensationalize folk culture and dialect. The story starts with comic incongruity. It opens in approximately 1818 with a troop of milkmaids, including one who is set apart from the others, Rhoda Brook, and 'an old milkman' dressed 'in a long white pinafore ... with the brim of his hat tied down, so that he looked like a woman' (Hardy, 1999: 45). Conversing amongst the cows they are milking in such a manner that it seems as if the cows are talking, they share their expectations about Farmer Lodge's new wife, Gertrude. She is rumoured to be beautiful, well-bred, and much younger than her husband. The first impressions of the milking troop involve their normative expectations about Mrs. Lodge's social category and character, her *virtual social identity*.

Farmer Lodge is the father of Rhoda's illegitimate twelve-year old son, whom she sends after Gertrude to gain more knowledge of her. Rhoda wants to know if Gertrude 'shows marks of the lady on her', her hair colour, her height, and whether 'her hands be white ... or are milker's hands like mine' (Hardy, 1999: 46–7). Rhoda is looking for ways in which Gertrude might be different from her, but also different from her virtual social identity. Her son confirms that she is 'A lady complete', with 'lightish' hair and a 'face as comely as a live doll's' (Hardy, 1999: 48) He is unable to comment on her hands, however, as 'She never took off her gloves' (Hardy, 1999: 49). Via second-hand accounts, Rhoda generates her own *virtual social identity* for Gertrude, and within a few days of her arrival 'could raise a mental image of the unconscious Mrs Lodge that was realistic as a photograph' (Hardy, 1999: 50). The opening scene, while concentrating on expectations about beauty, also hints at deformity, with the landscape and buildings foreshadowing the stigmatized attribute of the story's title. The milkers 'washed their pails and hung them on a many-forked stand made as usual of the peeled limb of an oak tree' (Hardy, 1999: 46). Rhoda's humble cottage has similar patches of bare thatch where 'a rafter showed like a bone protruding through the skin', hinting at the withered arm that has yet to appear (Hardy, 1999: 46). Rhoda's status as a fallen woman is stigmatized. Her separateness from her community is spatial as well as social. She lives apart from her community, and she sits in a different place when she is with her fellow milkers. Goffman (1986: 5) suggests that normals treat 'undesired attributes', in this case being an unmarried mother, as 'often of a supernatural cast'. Rhoda has been 'slyly called a witch since her fall', but took no notice of it, because she could 'never understand why that particular stigma had been attached to her' (Hardy, 1999: 53).

The story takes a Gothic turn when the *virtual social identity* Rhoda has constructed for Gertrude occupies her dreams as well as her daytime thoughts. The dream version of Gertrude, however, has 'features shockingly distorted, and wrinkled as by age' and Gertrude sits on Rhoda's chest like a Fuselian incubus (Hardy, 1999: 50). 'Maddened mentally, and nearly suffocated by pressure, the sleeper [Rhoda] struggled; the incubus, still regarding her, withdrew to the foot of the bed, only, however, to come forward by degrees, resume her seat, and flash her left hand as before' to display her wedding ring (Hardy, 1999: 50). Here, Hardy continues the play on gender fluidity that we see in the scene with the milkman dressed as a milkmaid, as Gertrude takes the form of a male demon rather than a female succubus. The gender play in the opening scene also hints at transition, where the gender-nonconforming milker talks of a time when 'I hadn't a man's wages', hinting at gender transition whilst talking about childhood (Hardy, 1999: 45). While Rhoda is associated with evil and has a damaged moral status, the gender-ambiguous milker challenges normativity through inclusivity, being neither set apart nor regarded as morally exceptional. Hardy disrupts the normative through Rhoda's fallen woman and witch status, through the cows who appear to talk, and through the incubus version of Gertrude.

Gertrude's arm changes as a consequence of Rhoda's tactile dream, where Gertrude as incubus suffocates and taunts Rhoda, and Rhoda defends herself by grabbing 'her antagonist's arm' and throwing her/them to the ground (Hardy, 1999: 51). Binaries are once again challenged here, as Rhoda understands her defensive action to be an expression of her jealousy. When Gertrude visits Rhoda, Gertrude reveals what she calls an 'ailment which puzzles me' (Hardy, 1999: 52). Gertrude shows Rhoda her arm, where '[u]pon the pink round surface of the arm were faint marks of an unhealthy colour, as if produced by a rough grasp' (Hardy, 1999: 52). Gertrude attributes the change to an unusual dream, and Rhoda realizes that the timing coincided with her own dream, but does not share this with Gertrude. Rhoda feels guilty, as she has become fond of Gertrude, though '[i]n her secret heart Rhoda did not altogether object to a slight diminution of her successor's beauty' (Hardy, 1999: 54).

Gertrude's journey from 'normal' to stigmatized is what Goffman (1986: 32) would call her 'moral career'. This is the process by which her identity and moral status are changed. During this period of transition, there are phases of socialization where the stigmatized individual enters '"affiliation cycles"' that oscillate between their own acceptance and rejection of the stigmatized category (Goffman, 1986: 38). Acquiring a stigmatized attribute can be difficult, Goffman observes, because we may not always identify with the social group to which we now belong. Gertrude consults her physician, but the impression of the four fingers on her arm will not heal. Given the connection between the women, the wound appears to be emblematic of the prior romantic relationship between Rhoda and Farmer Lodge. The imprint of the hand is a symbol of marriage and indicates Rhoda's claim. This link is emphasized by Gertrude's not minding the arm (she has no knowledge of Rhoda's former relationship and has committed no moral infraction) and Farmer Lodge's dislike of it. Gertrude suspects '"that it makes my husband – dislike me – no, love me less. Men think so much of personal appearance"' (Hardy, 1999: 54). Rhoda advises her to '"Keep your arm covered from his sight"' (Hardy, 1999: 54).

Goffman suggests that it is a common response for the stigmatized to wish to cure or remove the stigmatized attribute. In this section of his study, he mentions the numerous folk cures and religious interventions that people turn to, such as 'youth restorers as in rejuvenation through fertilized egg yolk treatment, cures through faith' (Goffman, 1986: 9). Rhoda takes Gertrude to the local cunning man, the uncanny Conjuror Trendle, even though she is concerned that he might reveal that she is the cause of the ailment. Trendle lives on the fringes of society, 'cloaked and veiled', and is, similarly, a stigmatized individual. He is initially thought to be dead, and the community believes that Rhoda is only able to find him because 'a sorceress would know the whereabouts of the exorcist' (Hardy, 1999: 55). The journey to find him is reminiscent of Lear's mad scene, as the women cross a heath in a storm, both realizing that seeking a cure in magic is not something that would be done by a woman of 'common-sense' (Hardy, 1999: 55).

Trendle determines that '"Medicine can't cure it"' as '"'Tis the work of the enemy"', hinting at the Devil, but also at a human antagonist, Rhoda (Hardy, 1999: 58). Trendle's egg-divination ritual reveals the culprit to Gertrude, which Gertrude never discloses. The community nevertheless assumes the disablement to have been Rhoda's fault. Hardy's story pits two belief systems (folk medicine and formal medicine) against each other, favouring the former. Folk medicine connects disability to a system of supernatural justice, where disability is a punishment in the case of a moral failure. Yet Gertrude is not at fault; her husband has committed the moral infraction. Gertrude is, then, the means through which her husband is punished. Farmer Lodge fears his wife's arm 'might be a judgement from heaven upon him' (Hardy, 1999: 59). The couple are childless, we are told, because Farmer Lodge is repulsed by Gertrude's arm.

With Trendle's guidance, Gertrude attempts a folk version of a saint's cure: to '"touch with the limb the neck of a man who's been hanged . . . just after he's cut down"' (Hardy, 1999: 61). This 'will turn the blood and change the constitution', Trendle advises (Hardy, 1999: 61). While waiting for the hanged body of an eighteen-year-old boy, Gertrude experiences an uncanny moment: 'a curious creeping feeling that the condemned wretch's destiny was becoming interwoven with her own' (Hardy, 1999: 65). Veiled, she positions 'her poor curst arm' against the victim's neck almost without will, as if it 'was held up by a sort of galvanism' (Hardy, 1999: 69, 68). This moment of bodily dissociation, compulsion, and veiling adds to the uncanny appearance of the scene. Rhoda and Farmer Lodge are unexpectedly in the room where the corpse is in its open coffin. They are distraught, because this is their son. Rhoda becomes the uncanny double of the incubus of her nightmare, 'clutching the bare arm of the younger woman, she pulled her unresistingly back against the wall' (Hardy, 1999: 69). Gertrude dies three days later (the ubiquitous supernatural Gothic three), and the narrator speculates that her blood had been turned too far. Her death becomes a catalyst for her husband's remorse, 'he eventually changed for the better, and appeared as a chastened and thoughtful man' (Hardy, 1999: 70). He dies two years later, leaving his estate to a reformatory for boys and an annuity for Rhoda, who refuses it. The story closes when Rhoda returns to the fringes of her community after a period away and continues her milking – a reminder, like the egg divination and the blood turning – of motherhood.

As in many stories about disability in the nineteenth century, disability is a curse or judgement for sin. Here the deaths of the stigmatized characters, Gertrude and the son of Farmer Lodge, and eventually Farmer Lodge himself, represent a parallel expunging of deviance and return to order. Gertrude is unable to move through the Goffmanian phases of socialization after acquiring a stigmatized attribute because her husband is unsupportive, and her rival's anger and jealousy is unresolved.

Goffman's place in Disability Studies is an important one as he recognizes that stigma is a disappointment in normative expectations – something that is central in the discussions of normalcy in the early years of Disability Studies theorizing. Hardy's study in stigma places two stigmatized women in a tense and unsettling relationship where they both attempt to negotiate their own understanding of their marginalized status. Their similarity is seen in their connections to the incubus figure, and the connections between the fallen woman and the deformed woman assists in linking deformity with a compromised moral status. The expert intervention, in the form of the cunning man, is catastrophic rather than heroic, and the normative expectations for female beauty clash with the realities of a deformed body.

2.5 Masquerading Bodies and W. W. Jacobs's 'Three at Table' (1899)

Tobin Siebers suggests that Disability Studies can change body theory, as the disabled body problematizes our understanding of the body. Siebers's (2008: 25) 'theory of complex embodiment raises awareness of the effects of disabling environments on people's lived experiences of the body', while accepting that some aspects of disability, such as 'chronic pain', come from the body. Disability, he suggests, is 'an epistemology that ... embraces what the body has become and will become relative to the demands on it, whether environmental, representational, or corporeal' (Siebers, 2008: 27). Siebers's idea of complex embodiment recognizes multifaceted ways of presenting and experiencing bodies, valuing disability as a form of human variation. Drawing on Goffmanian sociology, queer theory, and Critical Race Theory, Siebers develops the concept of passing to account for some of the unique ways in which disabled people present their disabilities publicly.

He calls the strategy of passing for able-bodied a *disability masquerade*. This form of passing manages the stigma of spoiled identities (Goffman), and passers are seen as people who 'recognize that in most societies there exists no common experience or understanding of disability on which to base their identity' (Siebers, 2008: 117–8). Masquerade is a version of passing that also resonates with the idea of closeting. The simple binaries of in and out do not work for disability, Siebers claims, because there are invisible disabilities. Siebers also draws on the understanding, from Critical Race Studies, that the heightened visibility of a stigmatized characteristic produces social invisibility. Disability passing is complex and takes several forms: (1) hiding a disability; (2) disguising a disability with another disability (e.g., using temporary-style crutches for a permanent disability); and (3) exaggerating a disability so that it is registered by others (e.g., an unnecessary hearing aid that warns people of the profoundly deaf). Attempts to pass create temporary or compromised identities that are costly to happiness, Siebers argues but have some social gain. He talks of his own exaggeration of a limp in order to make his disability more visible to those who may think he is unnecessarily boarding a plane earlier than people who appear to be able-bodied.

'Three at Table' is the final story in William Wymark Jacobs's collection *The Lady of the Barge* (1902), and is a Gothic exploration of disability masquerade. Best known for his stories 'The Monkey's Paw' (1902), a macabre variation on a three wishes narrative, and 'Jerry Bundler' (1897), Jacobs was an important influence on Edwardian Gothic short fiction. The son of a wharf manager at the London docks, Jacobs learnt his storytelling craft from sailors. His stories are studies in fear, and he often finds ways to humanize the monstrous.

'Three at Table' is told by an unnamed sailor who has been at sea for thirty years, but who has seen nothing strange while away. The fireside group of listeners expect to hear a nautical yarn, but the sailor explains that his most frightening experience was on land. While visiting his uncle, the sailor found that the family had not yet returned from the south of France, and so he stayed at the Royal George inn to await their return. He is the only visitor at the inn, and decides to go for a walk and have lunch at another inn. After a good lunch, he tries to find his way back, but is confused by a labyrinth of lanes and has to rely on his compass as he has wandered into the liminal territory of the marshes. The fog sets in and it gets dark, but the sailor meets a local who puts him on the right road and tells him that there is a village three miles away. He warns him not to go to the nearest house, as '"There's a something there . . . what 'tis I dunno, but the little 'un belonging to the gamekeeper as used to live in these parts see it, and it was never much good afterward. Some say it's a poor mad thing, others says it's a kind of animal; but whatever it is, it ain't good to see"' (Jacobs, 2014: 95). The path ominously splits into three, and the sailor is lost again and so calls at the house he has been warned about.

Anne, the old female servant, is noticeably unfriendly as she opens the door, but an old man, the master of the house, invites him in for dinner and offers a bed for the night. He explains that there will be three for dinner – the old man, his son, and the sailor – but that they will dine in the dark because his son's '"eyes are bad, and he can't stand the light"' (Jacobs, 2014: 96). The two appear to be unused to dining in the dark, however. The oddity of the behaviour of the members of the household and the apparent lie make the sailor uneasy and he accidentally upsets the fire screen while the old man is out of the room, and the additional light reveals that his son's face is scarred. The red glow of the fire prompts the sailor to doubt whether the son is human. Candles are lit, however, and the sailor is 'greatly moved' when he sees 'but the remnant of a face, a gaunt wolfish face in which one unquenched eye, the sole remaining feature, still glittered' (Jacobs, 2014: 98). The son is hailed as a hero injured rescuing several children from a fire. As they were celebrating the son's birthday that evening, the father tried to find a way to avoid having his son dine alone. The party, including Anne, drink a toast to the health of the rescued children and stay up chatting late into the night. Apologizing to the son for his reaction, the sailor explains, 'it was only in the dark that you startled me' (Jacobs, 2014: 99). The old man is sorry for the deception.

Aside from the story's modelling of acceptance, 'Three at Table' hints at the possibility that disability can disguise disability. This is not simply a way to closet the disabled body, but it is a purposeful attempt to avert the visitor's potentially stigmatizing gaze. The father's attempt to protect his son's privacy suggests an act of care that is also protective of his son's agency – a desire to be observed only on his own terms. The story is subtle in that the visitor recognizes the importance of contextualizing disability. The son's appearance is framed in several ways: by the local stories, the firelight, and the nervousness and inexperience of the family and guest. The visitor is sensitive that his fear may have caused offense and politely suggests that the deception and low light produced the suggestion of monstrosity, rather than his own prejudice. Jacobs's story begins with the idea of Gothic monstrosity, using disability masquerade to enhance the Gothic atmosphere and plot; but its wider point is about the dangers of the genre. A Gothic framing creates a harmful and unnecessary fear of deformity that gives way to a reframing where the same face can be read as heroic.

2.6 Conclusion

Gothic frequently asserts standards of beauty and fear of deformity, but not always in ways that reinforce the dominance of beauty standards: within Gothic, there are also reminders of the impossibilities of perfection, the artificiality of standards, and the cruelty of judging by appearances. Keats's *Lamia* navigates the pressures of beauty standards for women, where a snake–woman gains an ideal body to hide her difference, and ultimately removes herself from intrusive looking. In doing so, she echoes Frankenstein's creature, who disappears into a remote region. Just as Mary Shelley's creature searches in vain for people who can look at him without disgust or fear, so Jacobs explores the possibilities for disability agency by restricting the normate caller's visual experience of deformity. Jacobs is more optimistic than Shelley and Keats, however, allowing for the possibility of acceptance. Keats and Jacobs remind us that the moment where the Gothic body is revealed is a potent device. Coleridge uses it in 'Christabel' (1816), and Haggard in *She*, where the queen degenerates into an ape. Gaskell's 'The Well of Pen-Morfa' and Hardy's 'The Withered Arm', both set in rural communities at a time when these traditional ways of life were receding, use supernatural intervention and folk knowledge as powerful Gothic modes of resistance to the othering of deformity. Like *She*, these stories are concerned with disrupting normate-disabled hierarchies via idiosyncrasies of affiliation in communities of care. All three texts question embodied norms, particularly beauty and strength hierarchies, paying attention to the power of the gaze and the masquerading of bodies that are misjudged. They also rehearse the popular Gothic motif that the disabled body is a morally charged body.

3 Gothic Madness and Neurodiversity

According to Samuel Taylor Coleridge, most ghost stories can trace their origins to 'nervous excitation' (Allsop, 1836: 67).[31] We might also say that 'nervous excitation' is also often the subject of many ghost stories. Characters who see ghosts are often not sure whether they are seeing or hearing something that is a figment of their imagination, a symptom of an illness, or really there. For many Gothic writers, as Margaret L. Carter (1986: 1) has observed, 'a vision of a ghost is a very different experience for a person who believes in spirits and one who does not'. Carter (1986: 1) describes three possible consequences of supernatural encounters: a person 'must either revise his entire world view or consider himself the victim of a hoax or illusion – or worse, madness'. There are others, of course. Intoxication, for example, is popular (see Lock, 2023). This section will focus on madness and non-normative mental states both as a rational explanation for the supernatural, and as a reassurance that the supernatural is not present. Gothic madness is complicated by the problem of indefinability. Nineteenth-century accounts of madness are not stable. Melancholy, mania, and neurasthenia are some of the most common madness-related conditions named in Gothic literature, and the definitions of these are much debated by the doctors of the period. This instability raises important questions about diagnostic certainties. Disability Studies and Madness Studies foreground this uncertainty, troubling the authority of medical practice by asking questions about the kind of cultural work that a madness diagnosis does.[32] Elizabeth Brewer (2018: 14) suggests, for instance, that we de-centre the 'pathologizing of human difference' as the legitimate dominant cultural approach to madness.

The importance of madness to nineteenth-century Gothic means that madness is central to much counter-cultural questioning. Eve Kosofsky Sedgwick (1986: vi), for example, characterizes the archetypical heroine of the Gothic as a hysteric who endures 'an immobilizing and costly struggle ... to express

---

[31] The statement is a recollection from Coleridge's conversations.
[32] For a comparison of approaches to madness using Disability Studies and Mad Studies perspectives, see Donaldson, 2002; Brewer, 2018; Pickens, 2019; Donaldson, 2020.

through her bodily hieroglyphic what cannot come into existence as narrative'. Female fear is a hyperfeminine and disabling response, in which incapacitated women are rendered weak and vulnerable, and as such are often critiqued by feminist critics as replicating their patriarchal positioning or as predated by patriarchal figures. Gothic literature, as Diana Wallace (2013: 4) has argued, is also 'a way of symbolizing questions about history and gender which cannot be formulated in other kinds of language'. For Wallace (2013: 182), Gothic 'reminds us of the stark realities of historical abuses of women' in the asylum system. Additionally, as Scott Brewster (2012: 482) suggests, Gothic madness goes more deeply than character, however, arguing that 'Gothic does not merely transcribe disturbed, perverse, or horrifying worlds: its narrative structures and voices are interwoven with and intensify the apparent madness they represent'.

There are plenty of Gothic texts that place mad figures on display and that are, to a degree, complicit in exploiting the spectacle. Brewster (2012: 483) finds that 'Gothic at once objectifies and lives out the madness it encounters, striving for a metalanguage to categorize or explain insanity at the same time as it performs, even participates in, that very irrationality'. Mad narratives, such as Edgar Allan Poe's 'The Fall of the House of Usher' (1839), Brewster (2012: 488) observes, 'blur the boundaries between fact and fiction, reason and delirium'. While Gothic literature certainly evokes madness in problematic ways, it also opens up the possibility that there are alternative approaches to experiencing the world. Gothic literature is a space in which to imagine that a psychosis could be a shared reality, or that a vision that no one else can see could be understood to be really present.

In the nineteenth century, madness in an outdoor setting is often perceived as freedom, where individuals move beyond rationality to a state of elemental liberation. These settings are, however, also often places of danger. King Lear's madness finds its analogue in a storm on the heath, where madness becomes acute enough for the character to think about self-harm. The cliff-edge (which also features in *King Lear*) is a remarkably persistent trope in Gothic portrayals of madness that hints at a fatal and liminal boundary where characters are threatened with plunging into the chaos of the sea/mind. Mary Robinson (2000: 123 [ll. 25–7]) asks in 'The Maniac' (*Poems*, 1793), for instance, 'Why dost thou climb yon craggy steep, / That frowns upon the clam'rous deep, / And howl, responsive to the waves below?' Charlotte Smith's (1797: 2.11) madman, who teeters unawares on the 'giddy brink' of a 'tall cliff' by the sea, in 'Sonnet LXX' (*Elegiac Sonnets*, 1797), is envied by the poet as he is 'uncursed with reason' and does not 'know / The depth or the duration of his woe'. Cliff-edge madness signals a moment where mad characters are on the brink of insanity and caught in the boundary between extinction and freedom.

When madness is shown indoors, the focus tends to be on restrictions. Madhouses are disabling spaces, used in the Gothic to engage with ethical questions concerning care and agency, and with the arbitrary abuse of power. Gothic literature often explores the problem that being incarcerated in a madhouse and protesting against that incarceration can themselves be misread as madness. The lunatic asylum is as important to early Gothic as the castle, but its purpose is broader than that of the Gothic castle, which is a locus for patriarchal and aristocratic abuse. The Gothic asylum, as a space of terror, is about medical and systemic abuse.[33] The hauntings that we might see in the castle are replaced by hallucinations, or by the spectacle of the mad figure as ghost. Characters are often falsely accused of being mad and are wrongly imprisoned in asylums for the truths they are trying to tell. As the legislation on asylum provision developed in the nineteenth century, and care was gradually relocated from the community, the abuse of the process of diagnosis, and committal at all stages of the legislative changes fuelled fears about madness. These fears are Gothic fears. However, there are important exceptions to indoor (asylum and attic room) and outdoor (heath and cliff-edge) Gothic madness tropes. Poe's 'The Fall of the House of Usher', for instance, uses indoor space to signal the freedom to accommodate madness in one's own home.[34] And, sometimes, outdoor madness tropes involve pursuit as paranoia, such as in Sheridan Le Fanu's 'Green Tea' (1869).

3.1 Despair and Affective Disabilities in Mary Shelley's *Mathilda* (1819)

Ria Cheyne (2019: 1), in her discussion of the use of disability in affective genres, maintains that 'disability encounters are affective encounters', and that the feelings generated by these encounters are often difficult to understand. In genres that intend to elicit a particular emotional response, such as 'horror, crime, science fiction, fantasy, and romance', Cheyne (2019: 2, 8) argues, there are 'disability icons ... embedded within' that 'embody familiar narratives or tropes'. For Cheyne (2019: 17), disability functions 'within a larger affective system'. Disability Studies, however, as Cheyne (2019: 15) points out, tends to devalue 'affective, sentimental, and sensational texts', since they 'are perceived as manipulating the emotions, or as excessively emotive'. She suggests, nevertheless, that 'while genre narratives sometimes deploy disability in straightforward ways – to evoke fear in horror, for example', it is nonetheless 'more

---

[33] See Brewster, 2012; Noad, 2019. For an important account of the gendered dimensions of the history of psychiatric care, see Showalter, 1985.

[34] See Herrero-Puertas, 2022. For a wider discussion of architecture, Gothic space, and nineteenth-century literature, see Herrero-Puertas, 2020.

difficult than one might expect to find uncomplicated depictions' (Cheyne, 2019: 17). Cheyne invites us to consider '*reflexive representations* of disability: representations which encourage the reader to reflect upon what they understand about disability and potentially to rethink it' (Cheyne, 2019: 20. Italics in the original).

Elizabeth J. Donaldson and Catherine Prendergast are similarly concerned about the restrictive ways in which Disability Studies tends to view strong emotions.[35] They comment that, as Disability Studies has been 'forged ... with physical impairment as its primary terrain', it has 'inherited damaging ableist assumptions of "mind" that discourage a more robust consideration of emotion' (Donaldson & Prendergast, 2011: 130). Donaldson expresses concern elsewhere, too, that the co-opting of the madwoman figure as a paradigmatic 'feminist rebel' is 'an almost monolithic way of reading mental illness within feminist criticism and perhaps in the larger culture of women's studies scholarship' (Donaldson, 2002: 101). She argues that 'the madness-as-rebellion metaphor might at first seem like a positive strategy for combining the stigma traditionally associated with mental illness', but it 'indirectly diminishes the lived experience of many people disabled by mental illness' (Donaldson, 2002: 102). Donaldson stresses the need to examine the social causes and construction of mad identity alongside madness as an embodied material experience. These scholars make it clear that emotions need to be addressed within Disability Studies, and that disability in literature elicits strong emotions that work within affective systems that may be related to genre or to how that society treats emotion.

Mary Shelley's novella, *Mathilda* (1819), does not belong to any of the genres studied by Cheyne. Indeed, it does not fit easily into any genre, though there are elements of the Godwinian philosophical Gothic, with its references to necessitarianism, and of the morality of suicide. *Mathilda*'s oddity as a text – Shelley's father withheld it from publication – and its generic hybridity make it unsurprising that it explores affective disabilities in interesting ways. Much of the critical commentary on this novel has considered how and to what extent it is autobiographical and/or Freudian.[36] Kerry McKeever (1996: 192) reads Shelley's 'melancholy characters' through Freud, as 'plagued by their traumatic pasts' and by their primary narcissism, and as 'exhibiting primitive selves that are mutilated, fragmentary, and empty'. While criticism on this text has moved away from biographical questions, it does identify the work as written by

---

[35] See Goodley, Liddiard, & Runswick-Cole, 2018.
[36] See Nitchie, 1943; McKeever, 1996; Hoeveler, 2005.

someone who possibly felt these emotions, and so the writer may be from the disabled community.

Mathilda is a first-person narrative, dated 9 November 1819, in which the eponymous character tells the story of her life. Beginning with her current distressed state of mind, Mathilda traces her history up to this point, the root of which lies with her parents' education and with the loss of her mother. Mathilda's father is a man of rank, who is indulged as a child, and matures into a generous, but not self-depriving, man. Mathilda's mother dies a few days after she is born, and her distraught father leaves the country after a period of 'motionless and mute despair' (Shelley, 2017: 47). In his absence, Mathilda is brought up by her father's emotionally cold half-sister and a beloved nurse who dies when she is seven. In response, Mathilda treats Nature as a mother and books as companions. Her father unexpectedly returns shortly after Mathilda's sixteenth birthday; and, after the death of her aunt, she and her father move to London, where a budding courtship causes her father to become jealous and have periods of mania and melancholy.

Mathilda and her father next move to the family estate in Yorkshire, his former marital home, where Mathilda feels a strong connection with her mother. Mathilda's father, however, confesses to having a secret that plagues him with remorse and despair. Alarmed by Mathilda's accusation that he hates her, an impression formed in response to her father's emotional distance, and initially refusing to share his secret, her father suddenly reveals to her that he has inappropriate feelings for her. Mathilda is shocked and locks herself in her room. Her father leaves an explanatory letter, and, like Gloucester in *King Lear*, he heads for the coast to commit suicide. Mathilda pursues him, but she is too late and finds his coffin at a cottage near the sea. Fatigue and a storm contribute to making Mathilda ill with a fever. When she is well enough, she fakes her death and hides in a lonely cottage on a solitary heath, where she stays for two years.

Woodville, a young classically educated poet and son of a poor clergyman, finds Mathilda and befriends her. Woodville is also grieving, having lost Elinor, a beautiful heiress, whom he is not permitted to marry before she has reached twenty-one. Elinor died two months before her twenty-first birthday and twelve hours before Woodville returned to see her. As his friendship with Mathilda deepens, Woodville's unexpected absence during a storm causes a crisis that prompts Mathilda to offer him a suicide pact. He rejects this using broadly utilitarian arguments, as his mother and a close male friend depend on him. Called away by his mother's illness, Mathilda accompanies Woodville part of the way across a heath, on which she spends the night crowning herself with flowers in a manner reminiscent of Lear's crown of weeds and Ophelia's garland. The exposure to the elements makes Mathilda ill again, and she looks forward to her inevitable, and, as she sees it, innocent (because not self-inflicted) death.

Mathilda is a *reflexive representation* of madness that avoids pathologizing or creating a mad icon, but instead presents a number of non-medical or lay positions on strong emotions. Shelley is particularly interested in despair and its relationship to the more popular literary uses of madness. Despair is related to madness in the sense that it is sometimes identified as a symptom; but Shelley does not pathologize it as a medical condition. One can experience despair and still be regarded as sane. Eleoma Bodammer (2024: 320) observes of eighteenth-century German literature that 'the concept of despair [...] has been under-researched'. This is also the case for British literature. According to the *OED*, despair is 'a state of mind in which there is an entire want of hope'. Bodammer (2024: 319) notes that the brothers Grimm define despair (*Verzweiflung*) 'first and foremost as the highest form of spiritual pain and a state of hopelessness, the threshold beyond which there is nothing except the abyss, self-abandonment, or the deed that rescues the person'.[37]

Shelley traces Mathilda's journey into despair, but the narrative is not merely one of 'pity and tragedy', of which Donaldson and Prendergast are wary. *Mathilda* seeks what they seek: 'to address the tragic, the taboo, the painful, and even the mundanely unpleasant aspects of our lives' in ways that 'create an alternate space' for 'abject emotions' (Donaldson & Prendergast, 2011: 133).[38] In *Mathilda*, despair is to be learned from; and it is a yardstick with which to measure other difficult emotions. In her first encounter with her father's despair, for instance, Mathilda learns that it gives rise to 'wild thoughts', and that it gave her father an 'unearthly' or spirit-like quality that unbodied him: 'so tremendous were the ideas which he conveyed that it appeared as if the human heart were far too bounded for their conception' (Shelley, 2017: 56). Mathilda thinks of despair as 'an enchantment', a 'malignant vision' that has caused his metaphorical blindness, and she feels as if there is 'an unknown horror' at work that 'at times threatened to overturn his reason and to throw the bright seat of his intelligence into a perpetual chaos' (Shelley, 2017: 59). Mathilda's attempts to relieve her father's grief cause her to despair that 'each effort of mine aggravated his seeming madness' (Shelley, 2017: 59). When she empathetically records the emotional effects of the ebb and flow of her father's sadness, she notices that he contrives 'to nurse his melancholy as an antidote to wilder passion' (Shelley, 2017: 63). His cognitive behaviour in this moment suggests

---

[37] For a discussion of the political connotations of despair, see Schey, 2019.
[38] Summarising Scheuer, 2011.

agency and self-awareness, but also Shelley's willingness to decentre health or cure as the primary narrative trajectory. The instability of the emotions in this novel is also recognized as having interpersonal inflections. This is in the sense that strong emotions in one character affect another; but also in the sense that sympathy can ease emotions. Mathilda says to herself of her father, 'let him receive sympathy and those struggles will cease' (Shelley, 2017: 64). She also thinks that if she goes mad he will stop being suicidal, as 'my distraction might calm his'; but until she finds him after he exiles himself, she 'must force reason to keep her seat' (Shelley, 2017: 79).

Mathilda's descriptions of caring for her father while he experiences melancholy interspersed with periods of mania ('gusts of passion') find their meaning in a Gothic affective system (Shelley, 2017: 60). Watching his suffering, Mathilda encounters 'a horror that will not bear many words' (Shelley, 2017: 59). Within the affective system of the Gothic, emotions are as frightening as ghosts. When her father tells her he is 'on the very verge of insanity', Mathilda unwittingly pressures him to reveal his incestuous desire for her (Shelley, 2017: 67). This confession immediately causes in Mathilda a 'precipitate and irremediable change from happiness to despair' (Shelley, 2017: 57). It is also a Gothic moment. Her despair is vampiric and female,

> Yes it was despair I felt; for the first time that phantom seized me; the first and only time for it has never since left me – After the first moments of speechless agony I felt her fangs on my heart: I tore my hair; I raved aloud; at one moment in pity for his sufferings I would have clasped my father in my arms; and then starting back with horror I spurned him with my foot; I felt as if stung by a serpent, as if scourged by a whip of scorpions which drove me – ah! Whither – Whither? (Shelley, 2017: 69)

Mathilda's new reality after this moment is like life after a dream. Tearful and in shock, her emotions are so deep that she cannot determine their cause, and her memory temporarily blocks out the trauma. In the nightmare that she dreams that night, Mathilda's father runs away from her like a 'deadly pale' ghost 'clothed in flowing garments of white', until he reaches 'a huge cliff that over hung the sea' and she catches only the edge of his robes as he leaps down it (Shelley, 2017: 72). When Mathilda awakes, she reads his farewell letter, where he more explicitly articulates his incestuous thoughts and tells her it is better to 'have loved Despair, & safer kissed her' than to feel 'this guilty love more unnatural than hate, that withers your hopes and destroys me for ever' (Shelley, 2017: 76).

Later in the novel, Mathilda recognizes that there is a language of despair, and she internalizes this language by self-identifying as a personification of despair.

At the climax of the novel, where Mathilda contemplates suicide, she declares, 'I have learned the language of despair: I have it all by heart, for I am Despair; and a strange being am I, joyous, triumphant Despair' (Shelley, 2017: 104). Bodammer (2024: 319) notes that Judas, Cain, and Saul are often linked with religious despair. Mathilda similarly connects herself with Cain, and her father with Saul. Mathilda says: 'I believed myself to be polluted by the unnatural love I had inspired, and that I was a creature cursed and set apart by nature. I thought that like another Cain, I had a mark set on my forehead to shew mankind that there was a barrier between me and they' (Shelley, 2017: 107). Despair also has a disease analogue. Mathilda feels her soul to be 'corrupted to its core by a deadly cancer' (Shelley, 2017: 107). She realizes that dwelling on her father's revelation could drive her mad, and if she had become mad, this would have been 'a living pestilence' (Shelley, 2017: 107).

Mathilda is *reflexive* in its acknowledgement that emotions are not fixed, and that the descriptors applied to emotions change frequently. Mathilda describes herself and her father in multiple ways: manic, melancholic, and mad. Shelley determines, however, that despair is a component of a range of conditions, and shifts the focus away from diagnosis and mad-identities and towards to the particularities of feelings: 'I never was really mad: I was always conscious of my state when my wild thoughts seemed to drive me to insanity, and never betrayed them to aught but silence and solitude' (Shelley, 2017: 86). Shelley records the complexity and instability of emotions and self-identifying, as the characters exhibit a range of different kinds of behaviour that refuses labels. Suicide is the expected narrative here, as evidenced in the father's plot, but Mathilda leaves her death to nature, or to fate. The narrative resolves with a calm acceptance of death. At the end, Mathilda says, 'I no longer despair, but look on all around me with placid affection' (Shelley, 2017: 112). While the madwoman has been long understood as a metaphor for rebellion, Shelley here centres despair as a disabling feeling associated with the breakdown and loss of interpersonal relationships that traverses diagnostic labels, and in doing so she offers a reflexive and relational account of difficult emotions.

3.2 Performing Sanity in *Melmoth the Wanderer* (1820)

Peta Cox (2013: 100) suggests that 'theories of performativity' are as important for destabilizing 'the distinction between "being" and "acting"' in the case of sanity as they are for gender. Commenting on the interpersonal and contextually dynamic nature of sanity, Cox (2013: 100) remarks that 'passing as sane often depends on a person's embodiment, specifically how an individual's body is held, placed, and experienced by that individual, as well as how others interpret this embodiment'. Passing as sane involves mimicking sane behaviour, and this behaviour is culturally specific in the sense that 'one's sanity falls into question if one does not act appropriately for one's gender, race, class, sexuality, religion, and so on' (Cox, 2013: 105). Cox (2013: 108) destabilizes the notion of being mad, by presenting sanity as a performance, and arguing that it is possible to be aware of the expectations of sanity, and 'use the tension between acting and being as a way to manage ... symptoms or to maintain social engagement', while still being in 'distress'. In this way, Cox collapses the distinction between mental distress and mental health (acting and being), because one can identify as mentally ill on the grounds that one is self-consciously performing sanity. There are several kinds of behaviour evoked in Cox's chapter that enable one to pass as sane. These involve not responding to compulsions, mimicking norms, showing awareness of others' expectations, and planning (e.g., wearing occasion-appropriate clothing). There are, she suggests, unspoken rules about talking, looking, and movement that enable one to mimic sanity.

In Charles Maturin's *Melmoth the Wanderer* (1820), John Melmoth, a young student who inherits his uncle's Irish estate, finds a 140-year-old manuscript in a mouldy chest written by an Englishman named Stanton. Stanton has married a Spanish woman in Spain, and encountered Melmoth's demonic ancestor, also John, at the wedding. Stanton searches for Melmoth, but his ramblings about these events when he arrives back in England lead to a cousin committing him to an asylum. In order to pass as sane, Stanton determines 'to take the utmost care of his health and intellect that the place allowed', thinking that this would be 'the sole basis of his deliverance' (Maturin, 1989: 53). He washes regularly, gets up early, exercises, and 'with or without appetite, regularly forced down his miserable meals; and all these efforts were even pleasant, as long as hope [of release] prompted them' (Maturin, 1989: 53). As he realizes that his performance of sanity will not convince his keepers, however, he decides to neglect 'the means of realizing' his deliverance (Maturin, 1989: 53).

Stanton's time in the 'mansion of misery' gives him ample scope to reflect on the range of lunatics and the individuality of their cases (Maturin, 1989: 55). One woman re-enacts the trauma of failing to save her husband and children from a fire in London. There is an authenticity to her loss of reason that moves Stanton to observe that 'she was the only patient in the house who was not mad from politics, religion, ebriety, or some perverted passion; and terrifying as the outbreak of her frenzy always was, Stanton used to await it as a kind of relief from the dissonant, melancholy, and ludicrous ravings of the others' (Maturin, 1989: 53). He comes to appreciate the screams of the other inmates, listening 'with sullen and horrible pleasure to the cries of his miserable companions' as he becomes 'squalid, listless, torpid, and disgusting in his appearance'

(Maturin, 1989: 54). When the demonic Melmoth offers to deliver Stanton from his incarceration, Stanton refuses to compromise his soul in exchange for release. In his temptation of Stanton, Melmoth asserts that 'a time will come, and soon, when, from mere habit, you will echo the scream of every delirious wretch' in the asylum because 'the mind has a power of accommodating itself to its situation' (Maturin, 1989: 56). Maturin echoes a common theme in Gothic literature: madhouses make sane people mad. Melmoth characterizes this loss of reason as losing one's humanity: 'All humanity will be extinguished in you' (Maturin, 1989: 56). His ideas will become indistinguishable from ghosts: 'shut out from society, watched by a brutal keeper, writhing with all the impotent agony of an incarcerated mind without communication and without sympathy', Melmoth warns (Maturin, 1989: 56). Stanton will soon be 'unable to exchange ideas but with those whose ideas are only the hideous spectres of a departed intellect' (Maturin, 1989: 56). Ironically, given who he is, the demonic Melmoth presents madness as communing with hellish fiends. Stanton, however, maintains that he is sane: 'my sanity is my greatest curse in this abode of horrors' (Maturin, 1989: 57). Stanton finds himself unexpectedly free, though the reader is left to wonder how he escaped since he is liberated during one of the damaged manuscript's many gaps. Stanton's self-conscious performance of sanity draws attention to the distinctions between being and acting that Cox suggests destabilizes the notion of being mad. The fragmentariness of the manuscript, and the digressiveness of the narrative as a whole, supports Brewster's observation that Gothic madness goes beyond characterization and is part of the narrative structure.

3.3 Neurodiversity and Charles Dickens's *A Christmas Carol* (1843)

In the opening pages of *A Christmas Carol*, Ebenezer Scrooge asks of his nephew, Fred, "'What *right* have you to be *merry*? What *reason* have you to be *merry*? You're poor enough'" (Dickens, 2003: 42). Fred responds: "'What right have you to be *dismal*? What reason have you to be *morose*? You're *rich* enough'" (Dickens, 2003: 42). This parallel set of questions encapsulates a central issue in the novel: whether people have a right to express their personalities by acting in ways that appear to make them and others unhappy, and whether it is morally permissible to do so. And, by extension: is it justifiable for someone to intervene to encourage you to change your behaviour, if you are harming yourself and/or others? Here we will examine how our reading of Dickens's *A Christmas Carol* might change if we view Scrooge as neurodivergent, and the ghostly visits and excursions as a kind of cure. To make the case for *A Christmas Carol* as a curative narrative, I identify the characteristics of

Scrooge's personality and behaviour as indicative of Scrooge's neurodiversity, and especially his ways of managing stress. Scrooge appears, at least initially, to be coerced into undergoing the process of becoming sympathetic to poverty, and this raises some ethical questions over his ability to consent.

The issue of whether a disability is an acceptable feature of one's personality or requires correction is an important one for Disability Studies. The Neurodiversity Movement, for instance, supports a cultural shift away from a medical paradigm. As the sociologist and bioethicist Tom Shakespeare (2006: 109) observes, 'cures may be inappropriate responses to the challenge of disability, either because the person is not experiencing their difference negatively, or because barrier removal or social change would be a more effective response to their problems'. The concept of neurodiversity challenges the description of emotional and behavioural conditions solely as disorders to be healed or managed through medication and/or behavioural therapy. Autism, for instance, has been reconceptualized as a way of being that has its own strengths and advantages. Steven K. Kapp (2020: 1) defines a non-medicalized approach to non-normative behaviour as a move 'towards viewing' such conditions 'in social terms of human rights', and as identities, 'to accept, rather than as a medical collection of deficits and symptoms to cure'. The automatic assumption that neurodivergence needs cure, as many have observed, reinforces stigma and makes the choice not to be treated harder. Shakespeare (2006: 116) views neurodiversity as a particularly difficult case when it comes to questions about cure, however, and he calls for a balanced approach: 'the goal of promoting cultural respect and social acceptance for people with impairments should not distract us from the importance of mitigating or preventing impairment via individual medical or psychological therapies.' Shakespeare does not see medical interventions as being at odds with the cultural goal of removing stigma. The polarization of a medical model of neurodivergence against a social model of identity, it seems, is nevertheless becoming less of an either/or situation. As Kapp points out, the Neurodiversity Movement's aim is to balance a need for human flourishing and respect for difference with support for appropriate and consensual medical interventions.

When considering Scrooge's rights and reasons to be 'dismal' and 'morose', we could think about Scrooge's expressions of his personality in terms of neurodivergence. And, supposing that Scrooge is neurodivergent, I wish to explore *how* his cure happens, and the ethical implications of it, given that Scrooge is initially non-compliant. While it does not matter which conditions Scrooge may or may not have (these diagnoses change over time), examining which of his behaviours are marked for correction is important for understanding how Dickens presents normative personality types, and how non-normative behaviour is stigmatized.

Dickens centres on Scrooge's lack of sympathy, his solitariness, his anxiety about unexpected things, his hoarding and worship of money, and his frustration with the expectations that he should conform to behavioural norms. Although uncompassionate, Scrooge is not an unfeeling man, however. As his ex-fiancée Belle remarks, he fears 'the world too much' (Dickens, 2003: 72). Dickens describes Scrooge as shunning social contact and possessing a repelling energy. Beggars avoid asking him for money, and service dogs for the blind direct their owners away from him. He likes 'to edge his way along the crowded paths of life, warning all human sympathy to keep its distance' (Dickens, 2003: 41). Scrooge's concern about money derives from his fear of poverty. He also expresses a fear of intimacy. He dismisses marriage as 'more ridiculous than a merry Christmas (Dickens, 2003: 43). Aspects of his narrative hint at a fear of replicating a traumatic childhood.

Although Scrooge is unsociable and is avoided even by people who have never met him, he has a strong sense of the cultural work that normativity does. As his dismissal of empty displays of Christmas cheer suggests, he is particular about providing his own definitions of what he thinks is acceptable behaviour, and in assigning to others deviant roles. Ironically, given how Scrooge's own behaviour is viewed as deviant by other characters, there are many occasions when he finds the normative to be absurd. For instance, he describes Bob Cratchit as a 'lunatic' for letting charity seekers into the office on Christmas Eve. He regards Christmas as a time when people act out of character, spend money they do not have, and are happy in spite of harsh realities (Dickens, 2003: 44). Scrooge's meanness and his inability to sympathize have gone down in the cultural memory as his key characteristics, even to the extent that his personality before his encounter with the ghosts remains the archetype for the miserly curmudgeon.

While expressing these characteristics, however, Scrooge also demonstrates several cognitive and behavioural strategies typical of managing anxiety or stress. For example, he sticks to routines and uses verification rituals to calm himself (e.g., checking to see that the door is locked). He has the same meal almost every day. Even though it is Christmas Eve, he has his 'melancholy dinner in his usual melancholy tavern' (Dickens, 2003: 47). This is usually read as meanness, though it is not explicitly stated that this is the cause. The text supports a reading that Scrooge's need for the same meal is a part of his stress management. When things take a supernatural turn, Scrooge notably tries to predict the paranormal events, and makes certain that the ghostly visitors have left. Unexpected things, in particular, cause Scrooge a great deal of anxiety. To alleviate this, he tries to reassure himself by drawing on his cultural knowledge of what ghosts are supposed to do in haunted houses. These responses to managing unexpected stressors are typical of neurodivergent behaviours. The supernatural elements of the narrative disrupt Scrooge's expectations, often in seemingly gratuitous ways, and persistently focus on the circumvention of Scrooge's reassurances. For example, after Marley's spirit sets up the plan for the ghostly visits, explicitly stating the precise time the ghosts will arrive and the length of the period that will elapse between the visits (three consecutive nights), the scheme inexplicably changes. This discombobulates Scrooge. Scrooge's scepticism about the existence of ghosts at the beginning of the encounter with Marley, and his use of humour, similarly assist him in containing his fears.

Scrooge is further surprised when the ghost of Christmas Past appears, because, in his supernatural sleep, he has missed a whole day during which he was expecting to be awake. He assumes the ghost of Christmas Present will frighten him by drawing aside his bed curtains like his predecessor and draws them back himself, as he 'did not wish to be taken by surprise and made nervous' (Dickens, 2003: 78). But Christmas Present is late, and in the wrong room. Scrooge was 'prepared for almost anything, but he was not by any means prepared for nothing; and, consequently, when the Bell struck One, and no shape appeared, he was taken with a violent fit of trembling' (Dickens, 2003: 78). Unlike the previous two, the ghost of Christmas Yet to Come does not speak, covers his face, and communicates with a 'spectral hand' (Dickens, 2003: 102). This makes Scrooge anxious about interpreting the meaning of what he is shown without verbal guidance, and he is upset that the visions of the future are delivered out of chronological sequence. The unexpectedness of the final spirit's interactions causes a 'vague uncertain horror' in Scrooge' (Dickens, 2003: 102). Christmas Yet to Come surprises the reader, too, by appearing in the final lines of the previous chapter, instead of being contained in his own 'stave', like the other spirits, a moment that brings the anxiety to the level of narrative from

Scrooge's 'cure' centres on his socialization and the awakening of his sympathies. Taken back to his youth, he is reminded of his sense of abandonment when he was the last to be picked up from school; and of the grief he felt at the death of his sister and his sadness at the end of his engagement with Belle. His cure results in him discarding his routines and other coping strategies. He immediately gives gifts and celebrates Christmas with his family. He walks the streets engaging with people instead of avoiding them. His comment 'I don't know what to do!' suggests that he is free from his regular habits, as does his reference to being reborn (Dickens, 2003: 118). Scrooge continues, 'I don't know anything. I'm quite a baby. Never mind. I don't care. I'd rather be a baby' (Dickens, 2003: 119). His regression to an earlier stage of the ego signals his erasure of trauma. The unexpected no longer causes anxiety. Rather than shaking from fear, Scrooge shakes from laughing, and his new-found generosity signals the resolution of his fear of poverty. Scrooge's inability to replicate the traditional family is replaced by his rejuvenation as a 'second father' to Tiny Tim (Dickens, 2003: 123). By showing Scrooge what he is missing, and some of the possible causes of his lack of sympathy, the ghosts enable him to change. By the end of the process, Scrooge's new relationships replace his de-stressors, and he is made to feel grateful that he has been saved from himself.

If Scrooge is neurodivergent, and this is a tale about un/ethical intervention, then it is worth thinking about the criteria for informed consent, however. There are some unsettling moments in this story that indicate lack of consent. For instance, before he intervenes, Marley's ghost has kept Scrooge under surveillance. Additionally, the Ghost of Christmas Past, who has come for Scrooge's 'welfare' and 'reclamation', coerces him physically, and Scrooge's wish to stop is denied. Once he resigns himself to undergoing the process of change, however, Scrooge recalls that, while 'he went forth last night on compulsion,' he is now prepared to go voluntarily, though in trepidation (Dickens, 2003: 80). While Scrooge consents to accompany the next two ghosts, there is still evidence of coercion.

As the ghosts use physical force and have a coercive agenda, a question is raised over whether their intervention is justifiable. There is a standard formula that enables modern medical ethicists to assess informed consent. Informed consent requires that a patient's *condition* should not prevent them from doing the following: (1) *understanding* what they are consenting to; (2) *choosing* the intervention (3) *communicating* this consent or refusal, and (4) *accepting* the need for an intervention (i.e., accepting that the intervention is valid). There is, of course, much literature on the relationship between a condition and one's competence to consent. One study, for instance, suggests that past preferences are a way to gauge consent when a patient may be deemed unable to consent due to their condition (Rudnick, 2002: 151–5). Another method, and one which is closer to Scrooge's case, is a 'therapeutic trial', 'after which, if the trial is successful, the patient's competent treatment preferences can be established and compared to his or her preferences during' the time of compromised competence (Rudnick, 2002: 153).

In *A Christmas Carol*, we are told that Scrooge is grateful for the intervention after his cure, and so, if this is a case of medical ethics, it may be one in which he was unable to give informed consent before his treatment, and his appreciation of his positive outcome may be evoked retrospectively as a factor in making it ethically justifiable. An important factor in determining whether Scrooge needs treatment is the question of whether he is being harmed. Scrooge's nephew, Fred, hints that he thinks that Scrooge is harming himself when he pities his uncle by saying that his 'offenses carry their own punishment' (Dickens, 2003: 94). Fred encourages Scrooge to change, and his judicial language suggests that he thinks his case is serious. It is easy to overlook these questions of consent, as Scrooge's behaviour registers to most readers as meanness and selfishness. If we see Scrooge as neurodivergent, however, and his behaviour as an alternative way of being in the world, the case becomes more problematic than a one of normative etiquette or of teaching someone to be more charitable.

3.4 Mad Self-Advocacy and *The String of Pearls* (1846–7)

Stanton's declaration of his own sanity in *Melmoth the Wanderer* is a common trope in Gothic madhouse novels. In the anonymously published *The String of Pearls* (1846–7), commonly known as *Sweeney Todd*, Todd the barber has his apprentice Tobias Ragg committed to an asylum when Tobias finds out Todd is murdering his customers.[39] The asylum is 'a lonely, large, rambling old-looking house' with 'a high wall' surrounding it, that 'presented great symptoms of decay, in the dilapidated character of the chimneypots, and the general appearance of discomfort which pervaded it' (Anon., 2007: 165). Like *Melmoth*, the novel critiques the institutional power of the madhouse, where there is no way out and no way to convincingly perform sanity. As Benjamin Noad (2019: 178) has observed, mad characters are sometimes unexpected truth-tellers, and it is important to pay attention 'to the substance and contents of [mad] characters' speech that might otherwise be dismissed as insanity', as 'the Victorian Gothic encoded narrative truths beneath the pathological wailings of characters such as Stoker's Renfield'. In *Dracula*, Noad (2019: 185) suggests, Renfield's 'lunacy is actually a supernatural condition'. Noad (2019: 182) argues that 'the speech of madness becomes as struggle for ontological assertion'; and 'the mad patient screams their protests of sanity only to become mentally and physically exhausted by doing so'. He reads Gothic as 'uniquely empowering the voices of alleged madness' by questioning the medical authority of the institution and presenting 'madness as a suppressed truth, one that ultimately critiques and

---

[39] Robert L. Mack (2007: xxxi, xvi) notes that *The String of Pearls* has been 'variously attributed to Edward P. Hingston, George Macfarren, Thomas Peckett Prest, James Malcom Rymer, and Albert Richard Smith', and concludes that the attribution 'is likely to remain contested'. His edition for Oxford University Press is anonymous. See Mack (2007: xvi–xvii) for a brief overview of the scholarship on this question and Nesvet 2022. While Rymer and Prest (either individually or in collaboration) are the leading contenders, like Mack, I have opted not to attribute the novel.

questions the idea of what it means to be healthy, human, and homogenous' (Noad, 2019: 184, 188).

Tobias protests that he is sane. He is indeed telling the truth about Todd, but he is disbelieved because he is presumed mad. Tobias is, nevertheless, not presented as straightforwardly sane. His mother's ambiguous comment at the beginning of the novel, that her son has 'a little weakness of the headpiece' that disqualified him from training as a lawyer, may hint that he is not intelligent enough or that his sanity is already in doubt (Anon., 2007: 5). Tobias, before he is placed in the asylum, exhibits the characteristics commonly seen in literary portraits of melancholy. 'His cheeks were pale and sunken; his eyes had an unnatural brightness about them, and, to look upon his lips, one would think that they had never parted in a smile for many a day, so sadly were they compressed together' (Anon., 2007: 121). He adopts the melancholy thinker's pose, 'head resting on his hands, and looking the picture of melancholy abstraction', and 'he sits moody and alone' with his 'melancholy reflections', worried that 'I shall go out of my senses' (Anon., 2007: 122). When Tobias is waiting in his mother's house and is surprised by Todd, who grabs his head and turns it around to face him, Tobias shrieks and faints and is carried off to the asylum. The shriek is a common mad trait, and it is Gothicized in this scene: 'It was one of those cries which can only come from the heart in its utmost agony – a cry which might have heralded the spirit to another world, and proclaimed as it very nearly did, the destruction of his intellect for ever' (Anon., 2007: 162).

Tobias is committed to the asylum in Peckham Rye on the grounds of his assertion that Todd is a murderer. He protests: 'I am not mad; why call me mad, when the truth or falsehood of what I say can be ascertained so easily? Search his house' (Anon., 2007: 170). Tobias is caught in a paradoxical situation, as the madhouse keeper, Mr. Fogg, asserts that 'the strongest proof of insanity ... is the constant reiteration of the statement that he is not mad on the part of a lunatic' (Anon., 2007: 211). The reiteration is enough for him to be diagnosed as a 'monomaniac', or obsessive, demonstrating the imprecision in the medical assessment (Anon., 2007: 214). The narrator, however, protests that Tobias was sane when he went into the asylum, 'as sane as any ordinary Christian would wish him to be', but adds that, 'if by any ingenious process the human intellect can be toppled from its throne, certainly that process must consist in putting a sane person into a lunatic asylum' (Anon., 2007: 207). Tobias's youth and fancy (he is a boy 'of vivid imagination' to whom 'a mad-house must be invested with a world of terrors') makes him particularly susceptible, we are told, as adults have an 'enlarged experience' that enables them 'to shake off much of the unreal' (Anon., 2007: 207). Tobias's only way out is to escape, and he does this with the help of Mary, who recounts her own tale of her parents' committal of her to gain her aunt's legacy. Mary gives him access to her tunnel, tells him to make a rope from a quilt, but the rope breaks as she follows him over the wall.

The madhouse scenes in *The String of Pearls* dwell on systemic abuse, the use of torture and food deprivation, the murder of inmates, and the lack of proper oversight. All this is heightened by the use of Gothic spaces ('the gloomy dungeon-like cell') and soundscapes ('a shriek, and the lashing of the whips') (Anon., 2007: 207, 211). Mad self-advocacy is treated as symptomatic of madness and as a denial of diagnosis; and madness is a context that changes how words are understood. *The String of Pearls* continues this important self-advocacy thread in Gothic mad narratives; but it also keeps in play the subtlety that Tobias identifies himself, and is identified by his mother, who is a strong advocate for him, as mad.

3.5 Mad Queer: Cripping J. Sheridan Le Fanu's 'Green Tea' (1869)

Mark Sherry argues that disability and queerness share much territory. The overlap is not merely in the lives of queer disabled people, but in the 'experiential and theoretical overlaps' between disability theory and queer theory (Sherry, 2004: 769). Both Critical Disability Studies and queer theory problematize the social and biological, and critique normativity. Building on the Queer Disability Studies work of Robert McRuer (2002) and others, Sherry (2004: 778) notes that 'hegemonic heterosexuality is premised upon a lack of disability', or what McRuer identifies as a 'compulsory heterosexuality' that combines with able-bodiedness to produce normativity. There are several areas of common experience that Sherry identifies as overlapping in the formation of queer and disabled identities. For example, queer and disabled experiences of stigma and enfreakment; passing and coming out; and subjection to pathologizing. For Sherry (2004: 771), queer is not just an identity or about sexuality, it 'describes a certain critical relationship to heteronormativity'. Disabled characters can also be read as queer in the sense that their sexuality is often hidden. This overlapping perspective is known as 'crip theory', and it 'emerged as a particular mode of doing Disability Studies, deeply in conversation with queer theory' (McRuer & Cassabaum, 2021: np). The term 'queer-crip' signals the intersecting identities of queer and disabled.

In J. Sheridan Le Fanu's Gothic short story, 'Green Tea', the Revd. Mr Jennings, a quiet wealthy bachelor priest, is haunted by something that sounds like guilt. He is 'infected' with paganism (a shorthand for homosexuality), and his behaviour is perceived by other characters as non-normative and secretive. There is an unnameable oddity about him, 'a strange shame and horror'

(Le Fanu, 2008: 7). Jennings thinks, however, that he has a problem with his mind that can be cured by a doctor who investigates the paranormal.

The narrator of the story's frame is an unnamed translator who has qualified to become a physician but has not practiced medicine due to losing two fingers in a dissecting-knife accident and thence becoming ill. The narrator says that he has 'never been quite well since' and has 'seldom been twelve months together in the same place' (Le Fanu, 2008: 5). This dismemberment, with its hints at castration and deviance, along with his ill-health and wandering lifestyle, places the frame narrator in the margins of the story. This narrator identifies these experiences, furthermore, as drawing him to the narrator of the main part of the story, Dr Martin Hesselius, another wanderer. Hesselius is a playwright, interested in history, metaphysics, and medicine, who is introduced to Jennings by their mutual friend Lady Mary Heyduke. Lady Mary is fond of Jennings, and knows he has a 'carefully concealed' secret life (Le Fanu, 2008: 9). Whenever Jennings goes back to his vicarage in Warwickshire, Lady Mary reveals to Hesselius, 'his health soon fails him, and in a very strange way' (Le Fanu, 2008: 7). Hesselius's first impressions are that 'Mr. Jennings is a perfectly gentleman-like man. People, however, remark something odd. There is an impression a little ambiguous' (Le Fanu, 2008: 7). Hesselius guesses Jennings is 'unmarried' (Le Fanu, 2008: 10) and that he has a secret: 'I penetrated his thoughts without his being aware of it, and was careful to say nothing which could betray to his sensitive vigilance my suspicions respecting his position, or my surmises about his plans respecting myself' (Le Fanu, 2008: 9). A passing comment of Hesselius's causes Jennings a 'sudden embarrassment ... analogous to that which makes a young lady blush and look foolish' (Le Fanu, 2008: 10). There are further odd moments. When Hesselius later calls on Jennings, Jennings unexpectedly and uncannily appears behind him in the library mirror while Hesselius is reading a sexually suggestive passage of Swedenborg about evil spirits 'being ... conjoint with a man' (Le Fanu, 2008: 15). The *unheimlich* pairing of them in the mirror signals Jennings's and Hesselius's doubling relationship to each other, a likeness hinting at their queer sexualities. Jennings has marked several passages in the book about 'interior sight' opening up the ability 'to see things that are in the other life' (Le Fanu, 2008: 14). This queering of sight hints at the significance of the visions Jennings experiences: the visions are revelations of things that should remain hidden.

After several weeks, Jennings confides in Hesselius that he has tried living in the countryside, and has 'had a change of air, change of scene, change of faces, change of everything and in everything – but *myself*'; he has, nevertheless, not been able to remove his 'low and nervous' feeling, and places himself under Hesselius's care (Le Fanu, 2008: 19). Jennings reveals that just as he began to research paganism, he became addicted to green tea and started seeing visions. On the way back from buying some old German books, Jennings sees 'two small circular reflections' of red light at the front of the omnibus he rides home. They move to the level of the seat, disappear, and reappear. He next sees a grinning monkey. He prods it with his umbrella, and the umbrella goes through it. Jennings has a panic attack and then gets off at his stop. Left alone in the road, he briefly thinks he has escaped the monkey and is only about three hundred steps from his Richmond home. The monkey is, however, on a nearby wall, and its 'jaded and sulky' demeanour fills him with 'loathing and horror' (Le Fanu, 2008: 24). It keeps pace with him near to his left leg as he walks home. Jennings tries to comfort himself 'by repeating again and again the assurance, "the thing is purely disease, a well-known physical affection, as distinctly as small-pox or neuralgia"', or his digestion (Le Fanu, 2008: 25). The supernatural is more frightening than illness. The pathologizing of the spiritual turns the tables on the more usual Gothicizing of illness.

Jennings decides not to have tea that evening, and hopes cigars and brandy will chase the monkey away. It springs into the fire grate and up the chimney. Jennings is happy as it goes away for a month. When it comes back, however, Jennings thinks it is real and that it is dragging him to Hell. It now speaks, and will not let him pray, interrupting his prayers with blasphemies and urging him to commit crimes and injure himself and others. Hesselius visits him to try to help, lights the candles (a Gothic sign of rationality) in Jennings's house, and leaves for an inn with the devilish name of 'The Horns' to contemplate the diagnosis. When Hesselius eventually goes back to his own house, however, there is a note from Jennings, telling him the monkey is annoyed that he has consulted him and Jennings's servant has called three times. Hesselius rushes to Richmond too late, as Jennings has slit his own throat with a razor, having evaded his servant, who has checked on him regularly as instructed.

Hesselius diagnoses hereditary suicidal mania. In a letter Hesselius writes to his friend Dr Van Loo, he reveals that he has twice cured Van Loo of this illness, and has had success with fifty-seven other people. His treatment, however, is 'the simple application of iced eau-de-cologne' – a treatment that may well hint at queerness (Le Fanu, 2008: 39). Jennings's demonic monkey may have his origins in Darwinian concerns about evolution that fuelled religious doubt in the mid nineteenth century, as others have shown.[40] It may also show some influence of Poe's 'The Murders in the Rue Morgue' (1841), where the murder weapon the orang utang uses is a razor. In Poe's tale, the ape practices shaving, having watched his master. The ape's attempt at shaving may be hinted at in

---

[40] See Langan, 2011; Griem, 2014: 74.

Jennings's final moments, attempting to mimic normative masculinity. Le Fanu's queer–crip double-coded tale of spiritual torment overlaps the pathologizing of supernatural experience as suicidal mania with closeted homosexual behaviour. The more usual uncertainties about whether someone is mad or haunted posed by Gothic hide in plain sight a different question about sexuality.

3.6 Mad-gnostic: Elizabeth Stuart Phelps's 'What Was the Matter?' (1869)

As we have seen earlier, fictional madness often expects us to consider whether the ghost is either real or the product of a psychotic episode of some kind. When multiple people see the same ghosts at the same time, however, such as in Elizabeth Gaskell's 'The Old Nurse's Story' (1852), there is less ambiguity about the supernatural presence. Dickens thought that Gaskell's ending, where the characters all see the same ghosts, should be changed. He suggested that only the child protagonist should see them. This would have left unsettled the question of the reality of the supernatural. But Gaskell was adamant that all the characters should see the ghosts, thus validating child's view – the ghosts were real.[41]

Shared delusions, or *folie à deux* (the insanity of two or more), a diagnosis that was first established by Ernest-Charles Lasègue and Jules Falret in 1877, complicates this slightly. Lynne Piper Shackelford suggests that this is present in Poe's 'The Fall of the House of Usher', for instance. Shackelford (2017: 110) argues that Poe writes in the tradition of Ann Radcliffe, favouring 'the rational over the supernatural'; and so, for her, the rational explanation of the return of Madeline Usher from her tomb after an extended period without food or water fits 'the psychological reality of what today is termed shared psychotic disorder – in the nineteenth century, *folie à deux* – in which a seemingly healthy person shares delusions with one who suffers from a psychotic disorder, usually schizophrenia'. This diagnosis is, nevertheless, in tension with the supernatural.

Narratives can take on mad worldviews, or they can support the reality of the supernatural, or they can maintain that both are possible leaving us in an agnostic (mad-gnostic) unresolved space. The American writer Elizabeth Stuart Phelps connects mental and physical illness with an accidental and reluctant clairvoyant in her short story 'What Was the Matter?' (1869). Madness is presented here as a plausible alternative to the supernatural. Phelps was interested in Christian spiritualism (a form of clairvoyance that was regarded as compatible with Christianity). According to Roxanne Harde (2008: 350), 'Phelps sees in spirit manifestations further evidence for Christian

---

[41] See Gaskell, 2004: 344, n.10.

faith', but ultimately understood spiritualism to be 'a separate belief system and practice' due to 'its uncontrollability and capacity for evil'. Phelps's memoir *Chapters from a Life* (1896: 97) and her popular novel *The Gates Ajar* (1868) reveal that she associated the occult with grief, and particularly, with the collective grief of the post–Civil War period. She writes, 'Is there not an actual, occult force in the existence of a general grief?' Her short story covers similar ground, though on a more domestic than a national scale.

Phelps's narrator, Sarah Stuart, is a girl of seven or eight at the time of the earliest events of the story which take place in small-town New England. Her mother, a Queen-like widow who believes herself to be descended from the Stuart monarchs, hires as a servant Selphar, an impoverished local orphan girl of about twelve years old, when their long-time cook, Bathsheba, unexpectedly marries the local Sexton, late in life. Five years later, after 'a violent attack of diphtheria', Selphar 'slowly recovered, but her old stolid strength never came back to her' and 'severe headaches became of frequent occurrence' (Phelps, 2020: 59). Having gone to bed with a headache one night, Selphar comes down late after the family has managed to make their own breakfast, and is frightened, apologetic, 'and evidently undecided in her own mind whether she was to be hung or burnt at the stake' (Phelps, 2020: 60). The hint that she might be a witch is reinforced by references to her snake-like eyes, hints at possession (her eyes '*never looked at you*. Something behind them or out of them did the seeing, not they'), and the family's concern that her name is too close to sulphur, and therefore devil-like (Phelps, 2020: 66). Selphar uncannily does her chores that morning with her eyes shut, but is able to see: 'It could not be seen that she groped at all with her hands to feel her way, as is the case with the blind. On the contrary, she touched everything with her usual decision. It was impossible to believe, without seeing them, that her eyes were closed' (Phelps, 2020: 62). The family is amazed when Selphar retrieves a precious earring lost in the snow by Clara, Sarah's younger sister, and so they blindfold Selphar and test her ability with a pair of identical Bibles whose only difference is in the girls' names on the binding. Selphar determines which belongs to which girl. When Selphar later detects robbers approaching the house at night while on the opposite side of the building, Mrs Stuart decides that 'the girl is insane' (Phelps, 2020: 63).

Things come to a head when Selphar reveals that she knows the whereabouts of Sarah's mother's sister, Aunt Alice, who years before had been summoned by Sarah's imperious mother from the west of the country to come and live with them; but the train she was presumed to be on had crashed, and her body was not found. The family has mourned Aunt Alice deeply, keeping the bedroom she was going to stay in unchanged. Sarah's mother is outraged at Selphar's claim, and tells her daughter that Selphar is an imposter or 'self-deluded': 'How *can* she see, seven hundred miles away, a dead woman who has been an angel all these years?' (Phelps, 2020: 67). Sarah supposes that 'ninety-nine persons out of a hundred would have thought [Selphar] ... a candidate for the State Lunatic Asylum' (Phelps, 2020: 69). Selphar is 'haunted' by this 'delusion, if delusion it were', for weeks, and Mrs Stuart eventually takes the train to the location Selphar identifies, and returns with Aunt Alice. Aunt Alice dies shortly afterwards, having been forgiven for an unnamed indiscretion that forced her exile. After these many incidents of Selphar's clairvoyant fits proving to be revelatory, the family ultimately regards Selphar's condition as unexplainable, though the narrator offers the theory that her second sight is the consequence of 'the curious working of physical disease', and she mentions that the local doctor keeps notes on it, some of which find 'their way into medical journals' (Phelps, 2020: 69). Selphar's case is dismissed locally, however, as 'the fancy of "scared womenfolks"' (Phelps, 2020: 64).

Even though there is plenty of evidence that Selphar's clairvoyant insights are proved to be correct, Sarah's narrative persists with a rational explanation, even listing in point form 'a careful memoranda' of the facts (Phelps, 2020: 65). Phelps's story pursues a common subject in the Gothic: the conversion of the sceptic. In this case, however, the sceptics are left in 'a condition of simple bewilderment', rather than converted (Phelps, 2020: 69). Selphar's trances increase, and she becomes 'so thoroughly diseased in mind and body as to be entirely unfitted for household work, and, in short, nothing but an encumbrance' (Phelps, 2020: 70). After Mrs. Stuart dies and a new servant is hired, Selphar leaves without warning and is never seen again. Selphar's 'delusions' are both pathologized and treated as supernatural, with the story keeping in place the tension between these positions. The narrator's conclusion is simply: 'I have given you the facts. Explain them as you will. I do not attempt it, for the simple reason that I cannot' (Phelps, 2020: 70]. The sharedness of the mad delusions challenges the rationality of the narrator's worldview, and madness cannot explain away the supernatural because of its communality. The shared reality, then, could be a mad reality, a *folie à deux*; or the clairvoyance could be real.

3.7 Conclusion

Gothic both challenges rational certainties and offers madness as a rational explanation for the supernatural. It is a space for imagining that a psychosis could be a shared reality, even before *folie à deux* was a diagnosis. The authenticity of spectres and other supernatural phenomena raises questions that are as much discussions of the believability of mad characters who say they are sane as they are of the supernatural. Gothic's affective system includes a madness that generates fear; but we should also recognize that madness can generate reassurance, as it is the proof that the supernatural is not real. Gothic allows the protest of the person committed to the asylum to be made (though it is often not heeded), and for the neurodivergent to object to treatment; and it is interested in the paradox that protesting sanity is used to diagnose madness. Gothic Disability Studies has challenged the madwoman in the attic trope as a symbol of feminist liberation that deflects attention from disability, instead seeking knowledge that derives from being *reflexive* about how we understand disability.

4 Reclaiming Gothic: Concluding Questions

'Is Frankenstein's creature disabled?' is a question that does not have an easy answer. While 'disabled' may not always be the appropriate word to describe Gothic characters, it is possible that we can learn about the cultural positioning of disability from this Gothic mode nonetheless. Literary Disability Studies raises questions about the relationships between texts and their accounts of disabled bodies and minds in ways that can elucidate both.

We might ask: How are our ideas about disability shaped by Gothic traditions and conventions? We might also ask the reverse: How is Gothic literature shaped by our understanding of disability? Can disability help us understand the affective and effective power of the Gothic? How might Gothic literature demonstrate ableism or moments of disabled empowerment? What can Gothic embodiment and disembodiment tell us about disabled and accessible spaces? In what ways do uncanny, enfreaked, and monstrous bodies engage with discourses around spectacle, staring, and difference?

This Element has begun to reclaim Gothic by engaging with some of these questions in the context of nineteenth-century literature. I hope others will continue to answer them and raise more.

References

Primary

Allsop, T. (1836). *Letters, Conversations, and Recollections of S. T. Coleridge*. New York: Harper.

Anon. (2007). *Sweeney Todd: The Demon Barber of Fleet Street*, ed. by R. L. Mack. Oxford: Oxford University Press.

Darwin, C. (1871). *The Descent of Man, and Selection in Relation to Sex*. 2 vols. London: John Murray.

Dickens, C. (2003). *A Christmas Carol*, ed. by R. Kelly. Peterborough, Ontario: Broadview.

Gaskell, E. (1995). The Well of Pen-Morfa. In S. Lewis, ed., *The Moorland Cottage and Other Stories*. Oxford: Oxford University Press, pp. 123–43.
  (2004). *Gothic Tales*, ed. by L. Kranzler. London: Penguin.

Haggard, H. R. (2006). *She*, ed. by A. Stauffer. Peterborough, Ontario: Broadview.

Hardy, T. (1999). The Withered Arm. In M. Irwin, ed., *Wessex Tales: Strange, Lively and Commonplace*. London: Wordsworth Classics, pp. 45–70.

Jacobs, W. W. (2014). Three at Table. In M. G. Kellermeyer, ed., *The Monkey's Paw and Other Horrors: The Best Horror and Ghost Stories of W. W. Jacobs*, 2nd ed. Fort Wayne, IN: Oldstyle, pp. 93–99.

Keats, J. (1982). *Complete Poems*, ed. by J. Stillinger. Cambridge, MA: Belknap.

Lasèque, C. and J. Falret (1877). La Folie à Deux ou Folie Comuniquée. *Archives Générales de Médecine*, September, 257–97.

Le Fanu, S. (2008). Green Tea. In R. Tracy, ed., *In A Glass Darkly*. Oxford: Oxford University Press, pp. 96–124.

Lock, P. (ed.). (2023). *Dead Drunk: Tales of Intoxication and Demon Drinks*. London: British Library.

Maturin, C. (1989). *Melmoth the Wanderer*, ed. by D. Grant. Oxford: Oxford University Press.

Phelps, E. S. (1896). *Chapters from a Life*. Boston, MA: Houghton Mifflin.
  (2020). What Was the Matter? In L. Morton and L. S. Klinger, eds., *Weird Women: Classic Supernatural Fiction by Groundbreaking Female Writers: 1852–1923*. New York: Pegasus, pp. 51–70.

Robinson, M. (2000). The Maniac. In J. Pascoe ed., *Mary Robinson: Selected Poems*. Peterborough, Ontario: Broadview, pp. 122–6.

Shelley, M. (2017). *Mathilda*, ed. by M. Faubert. Peterborough, Ontario: Broadview.

Smith, C. (1797) Sonnet LXX. In *Elegiac Sonnets, and Other Poems*, 2 vols. London: T. Cadell and W. Davies. 2.11.

Secondary

Abram, O. (2022). Seeing and Surveilling: Ethics and Modes of Looking in R. L. Stevenson's *The Strange Case of Dr Jekyll and Mr. Hyde*. *Victorian Review*, 48(2), 309–26.

Aceves, N. (2018). Feminist Disability Studies Goes Goth: The Hyperability of Female Monstrosity in Charlotte Dacre's *Zofloya* (1806). *Studies in Gothic Fiction*, 6(1), 19–29.

Anolik, R. B. (ed.). (2010). *Demons of the Body and Mind: Essays on Disability in Gothic Literature*. Jefferson, NC: McFarland.

Barnes, C. (1992). *Disabling Imagery and the Media: An Exploration of the Principles for Media Representation of Disabled People*. British Council of Organisations of Disabled People. Halifax: Ryburn.

Barnes, C. and Mercer, G. (1997). Breaking the Mould: An Introduction to Doing Disability Research. In C. Barnes and G. Mercer, eds., *Doing Disability Research*. Leeds: The Disability Press, pp. 1–13.

Bodammer, E. (2024). Death by Despair: Destroying Health in Schiller's *Die Räuber*. In S. M. Hilger, ed., *The Health Humanities in German Studies*. London: Bloomsbury Academic, pp. 317–34.

(2025). Translating Disability: The First German Translation of Mary Shelley's *Frankenstein, or, The Modern Prometheus*. In S. Sati, S. Das, and B. Mahanta, eds., *Narrative Universes of Disability*. Singapore: Springer Nature, pp. 135–53.

Bolt, D., Rodas, J. M., and Donaldson, E., eds. (2012). *The Madwoman and the Blindman: Jane Eyre, Discourse, Disability*. Columbus: Ohio State University Press.

Botting, E. H. (2018). *Mary Shelley and the Rights of the Child: Political Philosophy in Frankenstein*. Philadelphia: University of Pennsylvania Press.

Brennan, Z. (2023). Old Age and the Gothic. In S. Falcus, H. Hartung, and R. Medina, eds., *The Bloomsbury Handbook to Ageing in Contemporary Literature and Film*. London: Bloomsbury Academic, pp. 103–14.

Brewer, E. (2018). Coming Out Mad, Coming Out Disabled. In E. J. Donaldson, ed., *Literatures of Madness: Disability Studies and Mental Health*. New York: Palgrave Macmillan, pp. 11–30.

Brewster, S. (2012). Seeing Things: Gothic and the Madness of Interpretation. In D. Punter, ed., *A New Companion to the Gothic*. Hoboken, NJ: John Wiley, pp. 481–95.

Carter, M. L. (1986). *Specter or Delusion? The Supernatural in Gothic Fiction*. Ann Arbor: UMI Research Press.

Cheyne, R. (2019). *Disability, Literature, Genre: Representation and Affect in Contemporary Fiction*. Liverpool: Liverpool University Press.

Chow, J. (2023). Desiring Deformity in the Romantic Gothic. In A. Haefele-Thomas, ed., *Queer Gothic: An Edinburgh Companion*. Edinburgh: Edinburgh University Press, pp 17–37.

Cohen, J. J. (1996). Monster Theory (Seven Theses). In J. J. Cohen, ed., *Monster Theory: Reading Culture*. Minneapolis: University of Minnesota Press, pp. 3–25.

Costa, S. (2019). Foreword: Disability, Metonymic Disruption, and the Gothic. *Studies in Gothic Fiction*, 6(1), 5–6.

Couser, G. T. (2001). Conflicting Paradigms: The Rhetorics of Disability Memoir. In J. C. Wilson and C. Lewiecki-Wilson, eds., *Embodied Rhetorics: Disability in Language and Culture*. Carbondale: Southern Illinois University Press, pp. 78–91.

  (2009). *Signifying Bodies: Disability in Contemporary Life Writing*. Ann Arbor: University of Michigan Press.

Cox, P. (2013). Passing as Sane, or, How to Get People to Sit Next to You on the Bus. In J. A. Brune and D. J. Wilson, eds., *Disability and Passing: Blurring the Lines of Identity*. Philadelphia, PA: Temple University Press, pp. 99–110.

Craton, L. (2009). *The Victorian Freak Show: The Significance of Disability and Physical Differences in Nineteenth-Century Fiction*. London: Cambria Press.

Davis, L. J. (1995). *Enforcing Normalcy: Disability, Deafness, and the Body*. London: Verso.

Delyfer, C. (2010). Lucas Malet's Subversive Late-Gothic: Humanizing the Monster in *The History of Sir Richard Calmady*. In R. B. Anolik, ed., *Demons of the Body and Mind: Essays on Disability and Gothic Literature*. Jefferson, NC: McFarland, pp. 80–96.

Deustch, H. and Nussbaum, F. (eds.). (2000). *"Defects": Engendering the Modern Body*. Ann Arbor: University of Michigan Press.

Dittmer, N. C. (2023). *Monstrous Women and Ecofeminism in the Victorian Gothic, 1837–1871*. Lanham, MD: Lexington.

Donaldson, E. J. (2002). The Corpus of the Madwoman: Toward a Feminist Disability Studies Theory of Embodiment and Mental Illness. *NWSA Journal*, 14(3), 99–119.

  (2020). Mental Health Issues: Alienists, Asylums, and the Mad. In J. Huff and M. Stoddard Holmes, eds., *A Cultural History of Disability in the Long Nineteenth Century*. London: Bloomsbury Academic, pp. 149–68.

Donaldson, E. J. and Prendergast, C. (2011). Introduction: Disability and Emotion: "There's No Crying in Disability Studies!" *Journal of Literary and Cultural Disability Studies*, 5(2), 129–36.

Durvbach, N. (2009). *Spectacle of Deformity: Freak Shows and Modern British Culture*. Berkeley: University of California Press.

Esmail, J. and Keep, C. (2009). Victorian Disability: Introduction. *Victorian Review*, 35(2), 45–51.

Esmail, J. (2013). *Reading Victorian Deafness: Signs and Sounds in Victorian Literature and Culture*. Ohio: Ohio Unversity Press.

Faas, E. (1988). *Retreat into the Mind: Victorian Poetry and the Rise of Psychiatry*. Princeton, NJ: Princeton University Press.

Farr, J. S. (2019). *Novel Bodies: Disability and Sexuality in Eighteenth-Century British Literature*. Lewisburg, PA: Bucknell University Press.

(2020). Crip Gothic: Affiliations of Disability and Queerness in Horace Walpole's *The Castle of Otranto* (1764). In A. Hall, ed., *The Routledge Companion to Literature and Disability*. Abingdon: Routledge, pp. 109–19.

Fiedler, L. (1978). *Freaks: Myths and Images of the Secret Self*. New York: Simon and Schuster, 1978.

Flint, K. (2006). Disability and Difference. In J. B. Taylor, ed., *The Cambridge Companion to Wilkie Collins*. Cambridge: Cambridge University Press, pp. 153–67.

Foucault, M. (1965). *Madness and Civilization: A History of Insanity in the Age of Reason*. New York: Pantheon.

(1975). *Discipline and Punish: The Birth of the Prison*, trans by A. Sheridan. London: Penguin.

Frawley, M. H. (2004). *Invalidism and Identity in Nineteenth-Century Britain*. Chicago: University of Chicago Press.

Gabbard, D. C. (2012). From Custodial Care to Caring Labor: The Discourse of Who Cares in *Jane Eyre*. In D. Bolt, J. M. Rodas, and E. J. Donaldson, eds., *The Madwoman and The Blindman: Jane Eyre, Discourse, Disability*. Columbus: The Ohio State University Press, pp. 91–110.

Gilbert, S. M. and Gubar, S. (1984). *The Madwoman in the Attic: The Woman Writer and the Nineteenth-Century Literary Imagination*. New Haven, CT: Yale University Press.

Gigante, D. (2000). Facing the Ugly: The Case of *Frankenstein*. *English Literary History*, 67(2), 565–87.

Goffman, E. (1986). *Stigma: Notes on the Management of a Spoiled Identity*. New York: Simon and Schuster.

Goodley, D., Liddiard, K., and Runswick-Cole, K. (2018). Feeling Disability: Theories of Affect and Critical Disability Studies. *Disability and Society*, 33(2), 197–217.

Gore, C. W. (2020). *Plotting Disability in the Nineteenth-Century Novel*. Edinburgh: Edinburgh University Press.

Gregory, A. (2018). Disability and Horror. In K. Corstorphine and L. R. Kremmel, eds., *The Palgrave Handbook to Horror Literature*. Cham, Switzerland: Palgrave Macmillan, pp. 291–99.

Griem, J. (2014). Gender Trouble as Monkey Business: Changing Roles of Simian Characters in Literature and Film between 1870 and 1930. In E. Voigts, B. Schaff, and M. Pietrzak-Franger, eds., *Reflecting on Darwin*. London: Routledge, pp. 73–89.

Halberstam, J. (2000). *Skin Shows: Gothic Horror and the Technology of Monsters*. Durham, NC: Duke University Press.

Hall, C. (2010). "Colossal Vices" and "Terrible Deformities" in George Lippard's Gothic Nightmare. In R. B. Anolik, ed., *Demons of the Body and Mind: Essays on Disability and Gothic Literature*. Jefferson, NC: McFarland, pp. 35–46.

Harde, R. (2008). "God, or Something Like That": Elizabeth Stuart Phelps's Christian Spiritualism. *Women's Writing*, 15, 348–70.

Herrero-Puertas, M. (2020). Gothic Access. *Journal of Literary and Cultural Disability Studies*, 14(3), 333–51.

  (2022). The Fall of the Accessible House of Usher: Poe, Berkoff, Neurodiversity. *Poe Studies*, 55, 3–31.

Hingston, K.-A. (2020). *Articulating Bodies: The Narrative Form of Disability and Illness in Victorian Fiction*. Liverpool: Liverpool University Press.

Hoeveler, D. L. (2005). Screen-Memories and Fictionalized Autobiography: Mary Shelley's *Mathilda* and "The Mourner." *Nineteenth-Century Contexts*, 27(4), 365–81.

Holmes, M. S. (2004). *Fictions of Affliction: Physical Disability in Victorian Culture*. Ann Arbor: University of Michigan Press.

  (2007). Victorian Fictions of Interdependency: Gaskell, Craik, and Yonge. *Journal of Literary and Cultural Disability Studies*, 1(2), 29–41.

  (2013). Disability. In W. Hughes, D. Punter, and A. Smith, eds., *The Encyclopedia of the Gothic*. Chichester: John Wiley, pp. 181–84.

  (2018). Born This Way: Reading *Frankenstein* with Disability. *Literature and Medicine*, 36(2), 372–87.

Holmes, M. S. and Mossman, M. (2011). Disability in Victorian Sensation Fiction. In P. K. Gilbert, ed., *A Companion to Sensation Fiction*. Hoboken, NJ: Blackwell, pp. 493–506.

Horner, A. and Zlosnik, S. (2016). No Country for Old Women: Gender, Age and the Gothic. In A. Horner and S. Zlosnik, eds., *Woman and the Gothic: An Edinburgh Companion*. Edinburgh: Edinburgh University Press, pp. 184–97.

Hudson, K. (2018). "Faking" Disability and Performing Gothic Narratives in Matthew Lewis's *The Monk*. *Studies in Gothic Fiction*, 6(1), 8–18.

Huff, J. (2008). The Domesticated Monster: Freakishness and Masculinity in Fitz-James O'Brien's "What Was It?" *Nineteenth-Century Gender Studies*, 4(2). www.ncgsjournal.com/issue42/huff.html.

Huff, J. and Holmes, M. S. (2020). Introduction: Negotiating Normalcy in the Long Nineteenth Century. In J. Huff and M. S. Holmes, eds., *A Cultural History of Disability in the Long Nineteenth Century*. London: Bloomsbury Academic, pp. 1–22.

Hughes, W. (2012). Victorian Medicine and the Gothic. In A. Smith and W. Hughes, eds., *The Victorian Gothic: An Edinburgh Companion*. Edinburgh: Edinburgh University Press, pp. 186–201.

Ingram, A. (1991). *The Madhouse of Language: Writing and Reading Madness in the Eighteenth Century*. London: Routledge.

Irving, R. J. (2022). Ann Radcliffe's Ruminations on the Ageing Body in *The Romance of the Forest* (1791). *Polish Journal of English Studies*, 8(2), 13–25.

Joshua, E. (2011). "Blind Vacancy": Sighted Culture and Voyeuristic Historiography in Mary Shelley's *Frankenstein*. *European Romantic Review*, 22(1), 49–69.

  (2020). *Physical Disability in British Romantic Literature*. Cambridge: Cambridge University Press.

Kafer, A. (2013). *Feminist, Queer, Crip*. Bloomington: University of Indiana Press.

Kapp, S. K. (ed.). (2020). *Autistic Community and the Neurodiversity Movement: Stories from the Frontline*. Singapore: Springer Nature.

Karschay, S. (2015). *Degeneration, Normativity and the Gothic at the Fin de Siècle*. London: Palgrave Macmillan.

Klages, M. (1999). *Woeful Afflictions: Disability and Sentimentality in Victorian America*. Philadelphia: University of Pennsylvania Press.

Knight, A. (2020). Mary Shelley's *Frankenstein*, Disability and the Injustice of Misrecognition. *Disability Studies Quarterly*, 40(4). http://doi.org/10.18061/dsq.v40i4.7109.

Kremmel, L. R. (2016). Suddenly Monstrous: Gothic Configurations of Disability and Justice in Joshua Pickersgill Jr.'s *The Three Brothers*. *European Romantic Review*, 27(5), 639–58.

(2022). *Romantic Medicine and the Gothic Imagination: Morbid Anatomies.* Cardiff: University of Wales Press.

Krentz, C. (2004). *Frankenstein, Gattaca,* and the Quest for Perfection. In J. Vickery Van Cleve, ed., *Genetics, Disability, and Deafness.* Washington, DC: Gallaudet University Press, pp. 1–12.

Kriegel, L. (1987). The Cripple in Literature. In A. Gartner and T. Joe, eds., *Images of the Disabled Images of the Disabled, Disabled Images.* New York: Praeger, pp. 31–46.

Lacom, C. (2005). "The Time Is Sick and Out of Joint": Physical Disability in Victorian England. *PMLA,* 120(2), 547–52.

Langan, J. (2011). Conversations in a Shadowed Room: The Blank Spaces in "Green Tea." In G. W. Crawford, J. Rockhill, and B. J. Showers, eds., *Reflections in a Glass Darkly: Essays on J. Sheridan Le Fanu.* New York: Hippocampus, pp. 313–31.

Lau, T. C. W. (2019). Chronic and Invisible: The Future of Romantic Disability Studies. *Keats-Shelley Journal,* 68(1), 136–7.

Liggins, E. (2000). The Medical Gaze and the Female Corpse: Looking at Bodies in Mary Shelley's *Frankenstein. Studies in the Novel,* 32(2), 129–46.

Linton, S (1997). Reassigning Meaning. In L. J. Davis, ed., *The Disability Studies Reader,* 3rd ed. New York: Routledge, pp. 223–36.

Logan, H. (2019). *Sensational Deviance: Disability in Nineteenth-Century Sensation Fiction.* London: Routledge.

Longmore, P. K. (1987). Screening Stereotypes: Images of Disabled People in Television and Motion Pictures. In A. Gartner and T. Joe, eds., *Images of the Disabled Images of the Disabled, Disabled Images.* New York: Praeger, pp. 65–78.

Mangum, T. (1998). Wilkie Collins, Detection, and Deformity. *Dickens Studies Annual,* 26, 285–310.

Marchbanks, P. A. (2010). Space, a Place: Visions of a Disabled Community in Mary Shelley's *Frankenstein* and *The Last Man.* In R. B. Anolik, ed., *Demons of the Body and Mind: Essays on Disability and Gothic Literature.* Jefferson, NC: McFarland, pp. 23–34.

Margree, V. (2018). The Victorian Short Story Forum: An Introduction. *Victorian Review,* 44(2), 163–66.

McDonagh, P. (2008). *Idiocy: A Cultural History.* Liverpool: Liverpool University Press.

McKeever, K. (1996). Naming the Daughter's Suffering: Melancholia in Mary Shelley's *Mathilda. Essays in Literature,* 23(2), 190–205.

McRuer, R. (2002). Compulsory Able-Bodiedness and Queer/Disabled Existence. In S. L. Snyder, B. J. Brueggemann, and R. Garland-

Thomson, eds., *Disability Studies: Enabling the Humanities*. New York: The Modern Language Association, pp. 88–99.

McRuer, R. and Cassabaum, E. (2021). Crip Theory. In *Oxford Bibliographies Online*. Oxford: Oxford University Press. http://doi.org/10.1093/obo/9780190221911-0109.

Miller, K. A. (2012). The Mysteries of the In-Between. Re-Reading Disability in E. Nesbit's Late Victorian Gothic Fiction. *Journal of Literary and Cultural Disability Studies*, 6(2), 143–57.

Mitchell, D. T. and S. L. Snyder (2000). *Narrative Prosthesis: Disability and the Dependencies of Discourse*. Ann Arbor: University of Michigan Press.

(2015). *The Biopolitics of Disability: NeoLiberalism, Ablenationalism, and Peripheral Embodiment*. Ann Arbor: University of Michigan Press.

Mossman, M. (2001). Acts of Becoming: Autobiography, *Frankenstein* and the Postmodern Body. *Postmodern Culture*, 11(3), 1–14.

(2009a). *Disability, Representation and the Body in Irish Writing: 1800–1922*. New York: Palgrave Macmillan.

(2009b). Representations of the Abnormal Body in *The Moonstone*. *Victorian Literature and Culture*, 37(2), 483–500.

Mossman, M. and Holmes, M. S. (2011). Disability in Victorian Sensation Fiction. In P. K. Gilbert, ed., *A Companion to Sensation Fiction*. Hoboken, NJ: Blackwell, pp. 493–506.

Nesvet, R. (2022). James Malcolm Rymer. *Oxford Bibliographies Online*. Oxford: Oxford University Press. http://doi.org/10.1093/obo/9780199799558-0165.

Nitchie, E. (1943). Mary Shelley's *Mathilda*: An Unpublished Story and Its Biographical Significance. *Studies in Philology*, 40(3), 447–62.

Noad, B. E. (2019). Gothic Truths in the Asylum. *Gothic Studies*, 21(2), 176–90.

Oliver, M. (1990). *The Politics of Disablement*. Critical Texts in Social Work and the Welfare State. Houndmills, Basingstoke: Macmillan.

Oliver, M. and Barnes, C. (2012). *The New Politics of Disablement*. Houndmills, Basingstoke: Palgrave Macmillan.

Orel, H. (1986). *The Victorian Short Story: Development and Triumph of a Literature Genre*. Cambridge: Cambridge University Press.

Pickens, T. A. (2019). *Black Madness:: Mad Blackness*. Durham, NC: Duke University Press.

Porter, R. (1987). *Mind Forg'd Manacles: A History of Madness in England from the Restoration to the Regency*. Cambridge, MA: Harvard University Press.

Punter, D. (2000). "A Foot Is What Fits the Shoe:" Disability and the Gothic Prosthesis. *Gothic Studies*, 2(1), 39–49.

Purinton, M. D. (2001). Socialized and Medicalized Hysteria in Joanna Baillie's *Witchcraft*. *Prism(s)*, 9(1), 139–56.

Reznicek, M. (2023). Haunting the "Proper Body": Disability, Contagion, and Citizenship in Irish and Scottish Novels of the Union. *Irish University Review*, 53(1), 48–67.

Richman, J. S. (2018). Monstrous Elocution: Disability and Passing in *Frankenstein*. *Essays in Romanticism*, 25(2), 187–207.

Roche, D. (2009). The "Unhealthy" in "The Fall of the House of Usher": Poe's Aesthetics of Contamination. *Edgar Allan Poe Review*, 10(1), 20–35.

Rodas, J. M. (2016). Autistic Voice and Literary Architecture in Mary Shelley's *Frankenstein*. In M. Bradshaw, ed., *Disabling Romanticism: Body, Mind, and Text*. London: Palgrave Macmillan, pp. 169–90.

Rosenberg, B. (1996). Teaching Freaks. In R. G. Thomson, ed., *Freakery: Cultural Spectacles of the Extraordinary Body*. New York: New York University Press, pp. 302–11.

Rudnick, A. (2002). Depression and Competence to Refuse Psychiatric Treatment. *Journal of Medical Ethics*, 28(3), 151–5.

Schaffer, T. (2021). *Communities of Care: The Social Ethics of Victorian Fiction*. Princeton, NJ: Princeton University Press.

Schalk, S. (2008). What Makes Mr. Hyde So Scary?: Disability as a Result of Evil and Cause of Fear. *Disability Studies Quarterly*, 28(4). https://dsq-sds.org/index.php/dsq/article/view/145/145.

Scheuer, C. (2011). Bodily Compositions: The Disability Poetics of Karen Fiser and Laurie Clements Lambeth. *Journal of Literary and Cultural Disability Studies*, 5(2), 155–72.

Schey, T. (2019). Romanticism and the Poetics of Political Despair. *ELH*, 86(4), 967–95.

Sedgwick, E. K. (1986). *The Coherence of Gothic Conventions*. New York: Methuen.

Shackelford, L. P. (2017). "Infected by Superstitions": *Folie à Deux* in "The Fall of the House of Usher." *The Edgar Allan Poe Review*, 18(2), 109–24.

Shakespeare, T. (1994). Cultural Representation of Disabled People: Dustbins for Disavowal? *Disability and Society*, 9(3), 283–99.

(2006). *Disability Rights and Wrongs*. Abingdon, Oxfordshire: Routledge.

Sherry, M. (2004). Overlaps and Contradictions between Queer Theory and Disability Studies. *Disability Studies and Society*, 19(7), 769–83.

Shildrick, M. (2000). The Body Which Is Not One: Dealing with Differences. In M. Featherstone, ed., *Body Modification*. London: Stage, pp. 77–92.

Showalter, E. (1985). *The Female Malady: Women, Madness, and English Literature, 1830–1980*. New York: Penguin.

Siebers, T. (2004). Disability as Masquerade. *Literature and Medicine*, 22(1), 1–22.

(2008). *Disability Theory*. Ann Arbor: University of Michigan Press.

Small, H. (1996). *Love's Madness: Medicine, the Novel, and Female Insanity, 1800–1865*. Oxford: Clarendon Press.

Starkowski, K. H. (2017). Curious Prescriptions: Selfish Care in Victorian Fictions of Disability. *Journal of Literary and Cultural Disability Studies*, 11(4), 461–476. https://doi.org/10.3828/jlcds.2017.35.

Sweet, R. (2022). *Prosthetic Body Parts in Nineteenth-Century Literature and Culture*. Bern: SpringerNature.

Tarr, C. C. (2017). Abnormal Narratives: Disability and Omniscience in the Victorian Novel. *Victorian Literature and Culture*, 45, 645–64.

Thomson, R. G. (1996). Introduction: From Wonder to Error – A Genealogy of Freak Discourse in Modernity. In R. G. Thomson, ed., *Freakery: Cultural Spectacles of the Extraordinary Body*. New York: New York University Press, pp. 1–19.

(1997). *Extraordinary Bodies: Figuring Physical Disability in American Culture and Literature*. New York: Columbia University Press.

(2009). *Staring: How We Look*. New York: Oxford University Press.

Tomaiuolo, S. (2022). *In Lady Audley's Shadow: Mary Elizabeth Braddon and Victorian Literary Genres*. Edinburgh: Edinburgh University Press.

Tromp, M. (ed.) (2009). *Victorian Freaks: The Social Context of Freakery in Britain*. Columbus: Ohio University Press.

Wagner, T. S. (2010). Ominous Signs or False Clues? Difference and Deformity in Wilkie Collins's Sensation Novels. In R. B. Anolik, ed., *Demons of the Body and Mind: Essays on Disability and Gothic Literature*. Jefferson, NC: McFarland, pp. 47–60.

Wallace, D. (2013). *Female Gothic Histories: Gender, History and the Gothic*. Cardiff: University of Wales Press.

Wallace, M. L. (2020). The Spector of the Singular Body in *Frankenstein*. In C. Mounsey and S. Booth, eds., *Bodies of Information: Reading the VariAble Body from Roman Britain to Hip Hop*. New York: Routledge, pp. 159–75.

Wang, F. (2011). Romantic Disease Discourse: Disability, Immunity, and Literature. *Nineteenth-Century Contexts*, 33(5), 467–82.

(2017). The Historicist Turn of Romantic-Era Disability Studies, or *Frankenstein* in the Dark. *Literature Compass*, 14(7), 1–10.

Warne, V. (2005). "If You Should Ever Want an Arm": Disability and Dependency in Edgar Allan Poe's "The Man That Was Used Up." *Atenea*, 25(1), 95–105.

Wasson, S. (2015). Useful Darkness: Intersections between Medical Humanities and Gothic Studies. *Gothic Studies*, 17(1), 1–12.

(2020). Spectrality, Strangeness, and Stigmaphilia: Gothic and Critical Disability Studies. In A. Hall, ed., *The Routledge Companion to Literature and Disability*. Abingdon, Oxon: Routledge, pp. 70–81.

White, S. J. (2010). Folk Medicine, Cunning-Men and Superstition in Thomas Hardy's "The Withered Arm." In R. B. Anolik, ed., *Demons of the Body and Mind: Essays on Disability and Gothic Literature*. Jefferson, NC: McFarland, pp. 68–79.

Youngquist, P. (2003). *Monstrosities: Bodies and British Romanticism*. Minneapolis: University of Minnesota Press.

Zigarovich, J. (2018). "A Strange and Startling Creature": Transgender Possibilities in Wilkie Collins's *The Law and the Lady*. *Victorian Review*, 44(1), 99–111.

Acknowledgements

Many thanks to Dale Townshend and Angela Wright for their wonderful support, to Richard Cross and Timothy Rhys Jones for their careful reading of the manuscript, and to Eleoma Bodammer for discussing some of these ideas with me. I would like to thank the students of my *Gothic Short Stories* class, my *Gothic* graduate class, and my various Disability Studies classes at the University of Notre Dame. Much of my thinking here comes out of these classes, and this Element would have been very different without our fruitful conversations. I am very grateful, too, to Talia Schaffer for inviting me to give a plenary at the Dickens Universe conference in July 2021, and for encouraging me to go with my hunch about Scrooge's neurodiversity; and to the Nineteenth Century Studies Seminar at the Institute of English Studies, University of London, for inviting me to present a longer version of my work on Scrooge in December 2021. Although our fields are different, my father, H. V. Joshua, continues to be an inspiration for all my academic work. This Element is dedicated to him, with love.

FOR MY FATHER

Cambridge Elements

The Gothic

Dale Townshend
Manchester Metropolitan University
Dale Townshend is Professor of Gothic Literature in the Manchester Centre for Gothic Studies, Manchester Metropolitan University.

Angela Wright
University of Sheffield
Angela Wright is Professor of Romantic Literature in the School of English at the University of Sheffield and co-director of its Centre for the History of the Gothic.

Advisory Board
Enrique Ajuria Ibarra, *Universidad de las Américas, Puebla, Mexico*
Xavier Aldana Reyes, *Manchester Metropolitan University, UK*
Katarzyna Ancuta, *Chulalongkorn University, Thailand*
Carol Margaret Davison, *University of Windsor, Ontario, Canada*
Rebecca Duncan, *Linnaeus University, Sweden*
Jerrold E. Hogle, *Emeritus, University of Arizona*
Mark Jancovich, *University of East Anglia, UK*
Dawn Keetley, *Lehigh University, USA*
Roger Luckhurst, *Birkbeck College, University of London, UK*
Emma McEvoy, *University of Westminster, UK*
Eric Parisot, *Flinders University, Australia*
Andrew Smith, *University of Sheffield, UK*

About the Series
Seeking to publish short, research-led yet accessible studies of the foundational 'elements' within Gothic Studies as well as showcasing new and emergent lines of scholarly enquiry, this innovative series brings to a range of specialist and non-specialist readers some of the most exciting developments in recent Gothic scholarship.

Cambridge Elements

The Gothic

Elements in the Series

Folk Gothic
Dawn Keetley

The Last Man and Gothic Sympathy
Michael Cameron

Democracy and the American Gothic
Michael J. Blouin

Dickens and the Gothic
Andrew Smith

Contemporary Body Horror
Xavier Aldana Reyes

The Music of the Gothic 1789–1820
Emma McEvoy

The Eternal Wanderer: Christian Negotiations in the Gothic Mode
Mary Going

African American Gothic in the Era of Black Lives Matter
Maisha Wester

Biography and the Trade-Gothic Author: The case of Isabella Kelly
Yael Shapira

Gothic Poland and British Fiction, c. 1790–1830
Jakub Lipski

Coastal Gothic, 1719–2020
Jimmy Packham

Disability and the Gothic: The Nineteenth Century
Essaka Joshua

A full series listing is available at: www.cambridge.org/GOTH

For EU product safety concerns, contact us at Calle de José Abascal, 56–1°,
28003 Madrid, Spain or eugpsr@cambridge.org.

www.ingramcontent.com/pod-product-compliance
Lightning Source LLC
LaVergne TN
LVHW011854060526
838200LV00054B/4332